# Grandad was a Sailor

## By

## Ed Dickinson, Master Mariner

Editor: Martin Warrillow
Designer: Carla Boulton

## INTRODUCTION

What follows is a factual account of my early career as a Deck Officer in the Merchant Navy, written in the earnest hope that my grandchildren will find time to learn something about me when they grow up, other than the hopefully fond memories of my darling June and our three sons becoming a little tired, when watching family television, of hearing the cry " been there!" from my armchair.

## DEDICATION

The very first person to whom I should dedicate this book has to be my dear mother, who religiously kept all my "blueys" and letters home during my time at sea and then gave them to me when I had learned enough sense to keep them. Without them, I would not have known where to start this book. She is closely followed by my lovely wife June, who has kept my feet firmly on the ground ever since I came ashore and given me three loyal and wonderful sons, Andrew, Simon and Jamie, who have made my life worthwhile.

## EXTRA THANKS

My grateful thanks go to all my old shipmates, our friends and neighbours in the places we have lived and, with very few exceptions, to all the people with whom I have worked in my years ashore, together with all my friends in the Merseyside Master Mariners Club, including our Padre, Canon Bob Evans, a prolific author, who has featured several of my stories, along with those of other members of the Club, in his books *Lantern on the Stern* and who has helped me with valuable advice in the production of my own.

# CONTENTS

# ANOTHER TIME - ANOTHER PLACE

## PREFACE

It seems unbelievable now that the Red Ensign was once flown by the biggest merchant fleet in the world and that British ships kept the world supplied with most of the goods required to keep people alive and in work.

Whilst the Second World War took a terrible toll on our fleet and the men who sailed in them, that war could not have been won without the munitions and food it was responsible for bringing back to the United Kingdom.

There were more men lost in the Battle of the Atlantic than in any other battle in the whole conflict. Even so, we still had the largest fleet once peace was declared, temporarily helped by the purchase of the American-built Liberty Ships, known fondly as the 'Sam Boats'. Whilst they were used mainly as tramp steamers, most British shipping lines acquired some for use in the liner trades until fresh tonnage could be built by the then-busy British shipyards.

This book covers my seagoing career, which extended between 1952 and 1962 when parts of the world were still quite primitive and ships not so sophisticated. Competition from fleets of ships flying flags of convenience was only just beginning to grow. These ships were able to be much more competitive due to reduced taxes and sometimes extremely lax regulation with regard to safety and qualifications, not to mention crew numbers.

At the same time, there were modern shipyards in Japan, built with the help of American money, which were blessed with extremely patriotic and hardworking Japanese workers. These men had never heard of demarcation and the yards in which they worked were starting to take a bigger and bigger share of shipbuilding business from over-confident builders on the River Tyne and the River Clyde. The British yards were more concerned with their labour problems than the low prices and more effective sales techniques being used by the Japanese. It all meant that our industry was beginning a huge period of change.

I feel extremely fortunate that I was able to ply my trade in a period of comparative world peace and yet see something of the British Empire before it quite rightly came to an end; to serve in proper ships, carrying interesting cargoes before they became huge floating boxes or tanks; to visit places before they turned into ports which look more or less the same the world over and finally, to spend time there and get a feel of how the rest of the world lived. Having got all of that out of my system, it was almost painless giving it up in 1962, particularly in view of the short leaves, which were still the norm. The nomadic life was more than compensated for by being able to live ashore, sharing a life with my lovely wife and seeing my children grow up.

So many of the older officers with whom I had sailed probably had similar ambitions but two world wars, with the Great Depression in between, had left them little chance to achieve those ambitions. This often appeared to have left them bitter, with only retirement to look forward to. Even then their life partner, after years apart, had probably made her own life which would leave little room for him. Retirement, in many cases, proved quite short. My story has a much happier ending.

# The Story Begins

## Chapter 1 - Hello World

I was born on May 8 1936 at the family home in Ormskirk, Lancashire. My first vague recollection, at about three years of age, would have to be laying in the road, unable to see.

Father had just changed his car from a small two-door Morris 8 to a Lanchester, which was bigger and had a door in the rear for access to the back seat. This must have represented a challenge, or perhaps it was the beginnings of an urge to see the world, which prompted me to climb off the seat and open the door before stepping out. As the car was travelling at around 30 mph at the time, this attempt at exploration was to result in a fractured skull and extremely worried parents.

Any desire to travel didn't extend to going to school which, from the age of five I always considered an unwelcome, if necessary, element of my life. For just over a year during the war my father, who had not been accepted for the armed forces due to a badly broken arm when young, worked for a construction company, on a beach site near Conwy in North Wales. They were building odd-looking barges out of steel and concrete which, when launched into the sea would, as we discovered later, be the first of many to be floated over the English Channel to become sections of the Mulberry Harbour and a vital part of the Normandy invasion during the Second World War.

At the tender age of 7, I was the only English boy in my class, attending a small school just outside the town wall at Conwy. The rest of the class chanting "t'was 'im Miss" and pointing at me, when I hadn't the faintest idea who had done what to arouse her displeasure, has remained with me as a bitter memory ever since. I was glad when we moved back to Ormskirk, where I attended a small preparatory school for boys until the dreaded 11 plus examination.

All people my age will remember the delights of that first banana and first ice cream after the war ended in 1945, although rationing was to continue for some time. School however didn't improve for me until my final years at the local grammar when a Mr Beck who, apart from taking a small band of us to Southport baths on a Monday evening for lifesaving classes, managed to enthuse me with mathematics, almost making up for the cold winter afternoons on the rugby pitch and French!

Without the distractions of television, and when not scouting, which gave me huge pleasure and a friendship outside school which was to last for life, my time was taken up with reading. The local library fed my imagination with stories of the sea by Conrad, Robert Louis Stevenson and Percy F Westerman. The adventures of W E John's flying ace Biggles, the Tarzan stories and Sherlock Holmes mysteries all involved foreign travel and contributed to a growing urge to somehow see the world; and in those days, the cheap charter flight holiday was not even a dream.

Another great influence on my choice of career was 'Uncle' Bill, our next-door neighbour, who was a ship's captain. He had been adrift in the Atlantic three times during the war after his ships were torpedoed and sunk, although I never heard him talk about it. Travelling to Liverpool, you could take a seven mile trip on the overhead railway from Seaforth at one end of the dock system to Toxteth at the other, giving a tremendous view of hundreds of vessels. Warships being repaired and stored ready for sea again and merchant ships with quayside cranes busy discharging and loading all kinds of cargoes. Beyond them you could even see all the ships anchored in the river, just waiting for a berth. The Port of Liverpool was so busy. It was after the war that 'Uncle' Bill and his wife Elsie were to take me on board his ship for tea and a "tabnab"(cake) in his cabin. I could hardly wait to leave school and to go to sea.

Sadly, two years before I sailed on my first trip, Captain Andrews ran his ship the 'Fantee' aground off the Scilly Islands in thick fog and was forced to retire from the sea, on a greatly reduced merchant navy pension. It seemed harsh that losing his ship in such a way would make any other British ship commanded by him uninsurable by Lloyds of London. This effectively made him unemployable, unless he was prepared to sail under another's command. With just a couple of years to go before being due to retire anyway, he took part-time work as a stand-by First Mate on ships in the port. So much for half a century of service and surviving two world wars at sea.

*SS Fantee. Vessel lost under command of 'Uncle' Bill!*

## CHAPTER 2 - ABERDOVEY

Before being accepted by the Elder Dempster Shipping Line, as an apprentice or cadet (or midshipman in some of the more "upmarket" companies !) I was required to attend a one-month course at the Outward Bound School in North Wales. Not at their expense of course and poor Mother had to fork out the fee of £20 plus the cost of a pair of stout walking boots. My course was, from September 20th to October in 1952, during a particularly cold spell of weather, or so it seemed.

Much to my shame, mother and father insisted on taking me to Aberdovey in the car and it took all my powers of persuasion for them to let me off at the railway station so that I could be met, along with other new arrivals, by one of the instructors. Even worse, they found accommodation at a small hotel on the road from the school down to the small jetty, forcing me to ignore them as we marched down to the sail loft each morning, where my watch "Raleigh" were assigned the job of rigging the sailing ketch "Warspite" with her sails. When asked by one of the other boys if I knew the couple who appeared so interested in what we were doing I shamelessly answered in the negative, without even needing to look and see who he meant. Thankfully they only stayed a couple of days and then left, apparently satisfied that I would survive!

In those days the Outward Bound School at Aberdovey was largely funded and run by Alfred Holt's, better known as the Blue Funnel Line of Liverpool, who also owned the Elder Dempster Line and, although the Warden and senior instructors were all professional, some of the others were seconded navigating officers. Many of the boys were, like me, poised to start a career as sea going officers although we had university students and apprentices from all trades amongst our number. I was to discover that even the galley staff were training for sea service.

Course 121 would last four weeks and we were split into watches, with each watch occupying a hut which we had to keep clean and tidy. Morning reveille was followed by a half mile run and then an icy cold shower. There was a row of about six shower stalls, each operated by a pull chain and the required full minute of torture was monitored by an instructor using a stopwatch, the minute not being started, or stopped until all six occupants had completed it. We started to learn that teamwork paid and it was remarkable how, although still virtually naked and barefooted, this treatment left us warm and glowing as we walked back, over the frost covered grass, to our huts. There we would complete our ablutions, before making sure that morning inspection of our quarters didn't win us any further chores as punishment. By 7.30 am we were ready for a hearty cooked breakfast in the canteen, after which there was a morning parade and we were ready for the rest of the day's activities.

We had all been issued on arrival with faded but clean, pressed, blue uniforms and after having our weight and height noted the following morning, the day's official activities started. These were all designed to promote team spirit but I was particularly pleased that my watch were to spend so much time on the sailing ketch "Warspite". The weather was quite calm for the first few days and Bo's'un Stan Hugill, an old shanty man from the days of sail, was in charge of the sail loft. Under his direction we rigged the masts and booms with the summer rig, only for the weather to change giving rise to fresh orders resulting in us having to change over to a heavier, winter rig, as each watch would hopefully have the chance of a short trip to sea over the coming month.

Bo's'un Hugill was quite a character, dark-haired and bearded, invariably wearing a long oilskin coat, complete in wet weather with a sou'wester hat. His booming voice was also used to good effect one evening a week when, instead of lectures, we were treated to an evening of sea shanties, before which he would explain exactly which job each was used for, as a way of helping the crew to pull together. His particular claim to fame was that he was the last of the shanty men, having served in this capacity on the last voyage of the last commercial British sailing ship Garthpool in 1929. Years later he was to be invited to conduct shanty evenings at colleges around the country. He was then persuaded to write a definitive book on the subject and I was fortunate enough to meet him, still at Aberdovey, some fifteen years after Course 121, when he was waiting for his second book to be published and showed me the proofs and long after that, to hear him singing his shanties in a programme he presented on the BBC. He was still involved in the Tall Ship races well into his eighties.

The first watch to have the pleasure of a trip to sea in Warspite had hardly crossed the bar of the river Dovey when a severe storm broke and, having taken shelter off Ireland they were eventually put ashore somewhere with an all weather harbour and arrived back at the school in a coach. They had almost all been violently seasick, the evidence of which covered their faces and clothes and the ship itself didn't appear back in the river Dovey for several more days.

This did not however dampen our enthusiasm for taking a trip and although the captain was not keen on taking her out again, he eventually agreed, in view of the work we had done getting her ready in the first place and the fact that the weather had eased. There was a permanent crew of the captain, chief engineer for the auxiliary diesel engine and one deckhand/cook and, together with Bo's'un Hugill we cast off early morning and motored over the bar before setting a course for Abersoch at the north end of Cardigan Bay. Sadly the captain judged that the wind wasn't right and we never did put any of our sails up before anchoring a few hundred yards off shore at our destination. We had a small wooden lifeboat on deck, which we launched and rowed to the shore, landing the captain and chief engineer onto a rocky foreshore, having been ordered to return later when we saw their signal. It was much later and quite dark when we saw their light and made our way back. It never occurred to us that it was just a little bit dangerous manoeuvring through rocks in the pitch dark but then, it was after closing time! We took turns on anchor watch in between managing to sleep in the fo'ç'sle accommodation, despite the smell of rotting seaweed from the anchor cable, tarred hemp and scorched silver paint peeling off the hot, galley stovepipe. We arrived back at the jetty later the following day, happy and satisfied with our little adventure.

We found out what the stout boots were for on the first Sunday at Aberdovey when we were taken on an eight-mile hike by Mr Fuller. Apparently an ex-Olympian canoeist he had earned the nickname of Springheel Jack due to the speed at which he could walk up steep hills. As we examined our blisters afterwards he made us laugh by saying that we would be doing 36 miles in a single day before we finished the course. Little did we know !! The following three Sundays saw the distance increased until on the final Sunday, when, before first light, teams from Beresford and Raleigh, the two top watches were put on a train to

Barmouth Junction. Given an ordnance survey map and compass, we were told to climb to the top of Cader Idris, the second highest mountain in Wales. There we met good old Springheel Jack, before starting the long walk back to Aberdovey. We arrived just after dark having walked 36 miles in the day.

Everyone was tested and graded in all the track and field sports, over the course, completed assault courses and generally kept busy all day, with lectures or shanty time each evening for the whole month. A final report was then completed for, in my case, my prospective employer where my strongest points seemed to lay in having good team spirit and showing stamina in the 5 mile walking race, although in my defence, I don't believe I had ever handled a javelin or shot in my life before! I came home by train, travelling with two other boys, from the Essex training school HMS Indefatigable, as far as Birkenhead where we separated and I took the Mersey Ferry across to Liverpool and another train home. |I felt fit enough to push our house down, never mind go to sea.

## CHAPTER 3 - TO SEA AT LAST

*On board MV Tarkwa prior to sailing
on first trip to sea*

Well, this was it! December 16th 1952, aged just 16-and-a-half, standing at the bottom of an impossibly steep gangway with a large cabin trunk full of all the items I had been told I would need; apart, of course, from the brand new blue uniform that I had on. This was the start of a four-year apprenticeship after which I would be able to start taking the exams needed if I was to become a Navigating or Deck Officer.

My father, who was convinced that I would be better suited to working in a local bank, had brought me to Liverpool Docks although it was my mother who had accepted that I was determined and who had helped and financed me to get this far. I was now on my own for the first time in my life, apart from at Boy Scout camps and the month I had spent at the Outward Bound School at Aberdovey.

I had been instructed to report to the Chief Officer on board the cargo and passenger ship mv Tarkwa and I quickly realised that to leave my gear on the dockside whilst I did so would not be a very good idea - so I left my father on guard while I climbed up to the deck to seek help. This soon appeared in the form of a ship's officer who, without a word, ran down to the quayside, threw the trunk over his shoulder and, just as quickly, climbed up again giving me the distinct impression that I would be more of a hindrance than a help!

He led me to the cabin up on the boat deck which would be my home for the next five months, equalling two round trips to West Africa and back. I would share it with three other apprentice deck officers.

I later discovered that this young officer was near the end of his four-year apprenticeship and had been promoted to what was known as an uncertificated Fourth Mate. This meant that, along with the more senior of my cabin-mates, he would take a central role in making me the butt of much humour during the course of my first voyage.

My ship was busy loading cargo when I boarded and for the next two weeks, I would spend most days down in the holds, watching the dock workers in a wholly unsuccessful attempt to prevent thefts. The following morning, dockers were already down in the hold when I climbed down the ladder at 8am and I assumed, when they trooped up the same ladder an hour later to be relieved by another gang, that they had been the night shift. I was surprised to see them return at 10am and made another, obvious but false, assumption that they had been on a meal break. Another gang change at 11am had me really confused and I had to ask one of the men what was going on.

He explained that there were two gangs to each hold and that they each worked hour about, spending the hour off in the canteen. I later discovered that this was known in the port as working 'the welt'. When I commented that this meant he was only working half a day I was told, somewhat indignantly, that he had spent three years in the Westen Desert fighting General Rommel and that he had done his bit!

More cargo watching, scrubbing decks and cleaning a dirty green fo'c'sle head bell until it was a handsome polished brass bell did not seem to be much like learning to be a ship's officer but I later realised that, when instructing someone else to do a job, it was much easier if you had already done it yourself!

Elder Dempster Line had also prepared for my arrival by arranging for a correspondence course covering all the subjects that I had to learn about in order to qualify as a Ship's Officer. It was only two months later, when we paid-off at the end of the voyage, that I found that I actually was in debt to the Company due to having to pay for the course.

A monthly wage of seven pounds and ten shillings "all found" did not go very far.

The Deck Officers, or 'Mates' had all started as apprentices like me, although some had been to various pre-sea colleges and were allowed to serve shorter apprenticeships. The Engineer officers had all served apprenticeships ashore in various heavy engineering industries but most of the crew seemed to have been in shipbuilding. We also had a ship's purser and a chief steward, who were officers. As the Tarkwa carried more than 12 passengers we also had a doctor, which may have had something to do with keeping the cargo in saleable condition during the days of slavery. If there were less than 12 passengers, it seemed that Ministry of Transport regulations did not require a doctor for the benefit of the crew!

Other ranks in the crew consisted of deckhands, who were normally signed on just prior to the ship sailing and were usually local men, in the charge of a boatswain or bo's'un and a carpenter who both reported to the First Mate. There were engine room greasers/firemen, normally taken on in Sierra Leone and the galley staff and stewards, who were Nigerian. This was apparently the result of some arrangement between the company and local government in order to provide employment in Africa, as well, I suspect, as a huge saving in wages for the ship owner.

All the Africans spoke English, but it was a version which would take me some time to get used to.

I was able to get a few evenings off in the fortnight that we spent loading cargo, duing which I used the good old overhead railway, affectionately known as 'The Docker's Umbrella' to get to a mainline station, from where I could catch the train home and then get back again in the morning.

We finally signed on articles and sailed on December 23 1952. Somehow, I was to spend the next five Christmases at sea during a four-year apprenticeship. However, despite my father's doubts, I was still keen for what the sea had to offer and enthusiastic for my new life - although, as the junior apprentice on board, this was often put to the test.

As an apprentice, or midshipman, flags became an important part of my life. They all had to be put up every morning and taken down at sunset. They were also taken down after putting to sea, except for the Red Ensign, of course, which is always flown to proclaim the ship's nationality.

It was duly delegated to me to take down all the other flags when we left the River Mersey. This was all going well until I discovered that the Company House flag, flown from the truck atop the main mast, had been jammed by the crew when hoisting the radio aerial. This was suspended between the top of the main and the mizzen or after-mast, to enable our radio operator to get weather reports and maintain contact with the rest of the world - satellites and e-mail were still well into the future.

I had always had a decent head for heights and reasoned that the simplest way to solve this problem was to climb up to where the halyard was jammed and to free it. As there was no ladder to the very top, this involved shinning up a stay for the last 10 feet or so.

Fortunately, I had just managed to get the job done before I was spotted by the Chief Mate on the bridge. My young ears were not then accustomed to the language he used, but I realized that I was being summoned and, after shinning down the stay again and climbing down the rest of the mast by ladder, I collected the offending flag and made my way up to the bridge.

It seemed to me to be just a bit unreasonable that, instead of being complimented on my initiative, I received a colourful dressing-down, during which I was told not to go aloft again. This was because the company's insurance did not cover anyone who went aloft with less than six months of seagoing experience - something which I had not been told, of course!

After that, things got worse given the bitter cold and rough weather as we made our way up the Irish Sea. Cleaning the stubborn green verdigris off the big brass bell on the ship's fo'c'sle when the ship was pitching in rough seas, or washing down the white paintwork with cold water and soda crystals, certainly didn't do a tender stomach or bare hands any good at all - yet no sympathy would be forthcoming if anyone was to expect it.

We were steaming north to Greenock in the Clyde in order to transfer cargo from another company ship which had broken down - this cargo consisted mainly of Scotch whisky and cases of bottled Guinness, with labels designed to celebrate the forthcoming coronation of Elizabeth II.

Every day, I was learning something new. If, for instance, a dockworker managed to drop a case of whisky hard enough for the bottles inside it to break, he simply needed to hold his billycan under the corner of the case, where it would catch the contents and prevent waste!

This was most apparent on Christmas Day, which was spent down in the hold, as it was not a public holiday in Scotland. For that, we would have to wait until Hogmanay, or New Year's Eve. Of course, we were back at sea by then, on our way to Africa.

Normally when we were at sea, the Deck or Navigating Officers and the apprentices would work watches of four hours on and eight hours off but, in fog and in the busy waters around the United Kingdom, extra eyes were needed. With radar still primitive and unreliable, it was common in these situations to double up on the bridge, with everyone doing four hours on and four hours off. Once we were clear of coastal waters, however, we were able to settle down to the normal routine of watches.

As the junior of four apprentices and there being only three watches, I was assigned to work on deck under the direction of the First Mate. This meant that I was also responsible for cleaning the cabin and bathroom that we shared, the good part of which was that I could stay in the warm until after breakfast. The bad part, however, was that if the Captain's inspection later that morning found any dust, or if all the brasswork wasn't gleaming and the floor polished, I was in trouble. After breakfast, it was back to washing paintwork or clearing scuppers until 5pm when, not wishing to see me idle, the Mate would summon me to the bridge, in uniform, for a couple of hours of extra watch-keeping duty until dinner.

The weather was still rough and it was still bitterly cold in the Irish Sea, remaining so until we were well into the Bay of Biscay. Things got much better as we neared the Canary Islands and we were in full white uniforms by the time we called into Las Palmas for oil fuel, still referred to as bunkers, even though our engines used oil rather than coal. We also started to see the ship's passengers on deck. I was certainly getting used to the gentle roll of the ship; the food was no longer sliding off the table and it was a pleasure to eat again.

It only took a few hours to take on oil fuel, but it was enough time for a local character called Frisco and his helpers to board the vessel and set up stalls, selling a range of local goods, some of the very rude variety, to the crew and passengers.

There was no chance for the crew to get ashore which was frustrating, as was the sight of boxes of butter and other items from our ship's stores being passed ashore, in a trade which must have been highly profitable to those responsible in the catering department. It was cetainly not in the same league as the pocket money we could make by selling the odd bar of soap saved from our rations.

However, we were soon back at sea and all this was forgotten in anticipation of arriving in Africa.

The normal life at sea is very much one of routine. The crew are split into day-workers and watch-keepers, both on deck and down in the engine room. Well away from land and with the finer visibility and fewer sightings of other ships, the other apprentices were taken off watches and assigned to day work which started at 7am.

The others started working on deck, while I had to continue cleaning our cabin. After breakfast I would join them, working under the Bo's'n until finishing time at 5pm, unless the Mate found some extra work for me, which he often did.

All meals were taken in the saloon, which meant getting cleaned up and into uniform before it was back into working clothes to gain more practical experience working with the crew on deck.

On the outward voyage, this consisted of overhauling all the running gear that was used to load and unload the ship, ready for arrival at the first discharge port in West Africa. The topping lift of every derrick had to be lowered to the deck and wires and blocks stripped, checked for damage, greased and hauled back up the mast to be refitted using the deck winches. All the running gear and guy wires were given the same treatment, with the wires changed end for end and eyes re-spliced where necessary, to ensure that cargo could be worked safely and efficiently. There were no shore cranes where we were going, so everything had to be perfect.

I was shown how to do a Liverpool splice in wire rope, using a marlin spike with a hammer and cold chisel to trim the ends, before seizing them with tarred hemp to protect bare hands; how to use a handy billy (a simple block and tackle) and what safe working loads were.

These lessons were important training for the serious business of life at sea; but there were some which were less serious. After visiting every department in the search for a 'long stand,' I discovered that, instead of being something we needed to hold the wire firm whilst we worked, it was a means of entertaining the crew at the naivete of the first-tripper. I also undertook a completely fruitless search before the keys to the keelson before I realised that it was part of the steel stiffening of the ship's hull.

After that one, I finally learned not to totally trust my shipmates.

As we neared land again, we had to resume watches and often, in the evenings and at weekends, I would be called to the bridge to act as an extra pair of eyes. The Chief Officer would spend some time instructing me in such things as the rules for prevention of collisions at sea and simple navigation, until the light started to go at which point it was back to being on lookout. This all seemed to leave little time to attend to my correspondence course!

The Company were the official mail-line from the United Kingdom to West Africa. They owned three medium-sized passenger ships which undertook a 30-day round trip with the addition of two intermediate mail boats, which included my ship, the MV Tarkwa, which carried up to forty passengers. It would take us about two months to complete the trip, as we also carried a full cargo of about 7,000 tons, taking a full range of general cargo such as machine items, tinned foods and manufactured goods out to Africa with large items such as barges and even rolling stock on deck, then bringing home the raw materials, such as groundnuts, palm kernels, copper, tin and latex to keep Britain's factories going.

The fine weather off North Africa encouraged our passengers to appear on deck where they seemed quite happy to enjoy the rest, as this was not a cruise for them but merely the first part of what would normally be a two-year tour of work - all would be travelling to jobs in the colonies. A considerable number would be priests or nuns, destined to do God's work in the more remote regions of Nigeria, Sierra Leone or what was then still called the Gold Coast.

Freetown, in Sierra Leone, was our first port of call. Apart from the discharge of part of our cargo, we would sign on about fifty Kroo tribesmen, who would work down in the holds when we were in port and chip rust off the decks when we were at sea. They joined the ship, each carrying a camp bed or mattress, together with a bucket and small wood bowl, containing soap for their strip-wash at the end of each day.

They would sleep under large canvas tents erected over the hatch covers. The same tents would be used during heavy rain to protect the cargo when the hatches were open in port. Answering to the collective name of 'Kroo Boys' they spoke in the same pidgin English as everyone in the old English colonies where, indeed, it was the only common language. I soon got used to them begging for cigarettes or other items and to their cheerful acceptance of refusal, as long as it came with a smile.

Our arrival at Freetown was looked forward to by most of the crew, as it was usually the first port at which we would receive mail from home. The temperature there was also much hotter than when we were at sea, so no-one minded that the stay was brief.

Back at sea, the ship's carpenter constructed a small pool on the boat deck, using canvas and large pieces of timber, where we could cool off during the hot days. We were also now starting to see lots of porpoise who seemed to take delight in racing alongside us and leaping gracefully in and out of the water in unison. They also seemed to like swimming immediately in front of our stem with their tails almost touching before shooting off to the side as if chasing the flying fish, which took off and skimmed to safety as we approached.

Arrival at ports was always timed for first light to allow for a full day of work; it was then that I was introduced to a normal working day in port. This involved unlocking the six hatches, with an average of five locking bars on each hatch, all ready for cargo work to start at 7am. Then it was back to cargo-watching in the holds which contained the more desirable items, such as tinned food or cases of bottled beer.

If this wasn't done properly, the workers would consume the goods there and then, resulting in both a spoilt cargo and a sleepy or drunk workforce - just like being at home, really, except for the heat and the more colourful faces!

It was only a short trip from Freetown to our next discharge port of Accra, in Ghana. Actually, 'port' was a bit of a misnomer because we could only anchor over half-a-mile offshore and offload our cargo, which was mainly bags of cement destined for the new port of Tema, which was being built just down the coast by the British construction company, Costain.

This cement had to be discharged into surf-boats, each carrying one sling weighing a ton-and-a-half. The eight-man crews would often fight over each boat, as they were paid by the load. These were Africans from upcountry, who appeared to have no garments other than a single piece of cloth which they folded neatly over the gunwale to sit on as they paddled, or wore as a loincloth or sun-hat depending upon which seemed the more appropriate at the time.

They expertly paddled to a beat provided by the helmsman clicking two shells together as he sculled with a steering oar at the stern. When the boat grounded on the beach, they would carry the bags of cement through the surf on their heads to keep them dry. I was told that, apart from a few shillings to spend each week, these men would be paid the bulk of their wages at the end of a six-month stint of work before they returned to their villages - I also heard that many would be robbed along the way.

When the Company Agent visited, he would be carried through the surf in style on a large chair which would take the place of a sling of cargo, so that he could be brought to the ship in the same way. Seeing and experiencing all this was what I had come to sea for.

Still on the Gold Coast, which was later to be renamed Ghana, our next stop was the more civilised port of Takoradi where we berthed inside the breakwater, or tied up at buoys inside it, whilst our cargo was discharged into lighters which lay alongside.

Sadly, this also meant that we were more vulnerable to thieves, so it was back to the old routine of cargo-watching. We would be relieved by one of the ship's officers for 30 minutes at lunchtime, when we were expected to get washed and changed into white uniform before dashing into the dining saloon to find that there was little time left for eating.

There was a similar break for dinner in the evening, with the only difference that we had to wear 'No 10's' consisting of a white tunic, epaulettes and long white trousers. This took less time, as we only had to wash our hands and faces before getting changed, thus leaving more time for eating! Needless to say, however, our white uniforms became dirtier on the inside than on the outside.

Fortunately, along with the Kroo Boys we had also gained laundrymen, or 'dhobi' men. It was somewhat less fortunate they could never be persuaded to go easy on the starch, which meant that our No 10s were sometimes able to stand up by themselves when we got them back.

I don't remember exactly how we did it, but some of us managed a couple of afternoons off to play football against another ship's team and the Takoradi European Club, games which were kindly organised by the padre from the local Flying Angel Seamen's Mission and our local agent. We could only manage about 20 minutes each way in the heat, but I suppose it was all good for crew morale.

Hatches had to be cleared and unlocked well before 7am to allow them to be opened for work to start, which meant that we had to be out of bed at 6am. These were long and exhausting days and when work finished at 11pm, there was a rush to lock all the hatches again before the canvas tents were erected, allowing the Kroo Boys to prepare their sleeping arrangements. It would be midnight before we were off-duty, but failure to secure the hatches would allow all kinds of mischief to occur during the night!

At last we had time for a shower, preferably a cold one; because we were floating on water and living in a steel box with no air-conditioning, the body's cooling process was slower than if we were on land. Our cabins remained oppressively hot and perspiration soon dampened the bedclothes but, not to worry, it would only be a few hours before it was time for the working day to start all over again.

We received our itinerary for loading just before leaving Takoradi on the short sea passage to Lome in French Togoland (now the Republic of Togo), where it was strange to hear the locals speaking French. I couldn't help but wonder if it was a kind of pidgin French and wished I had got a better grasp of that language when I was at school. This was only another short stop, however. We still had two ports to go in Nigeria before we would finish discharging our cargo. The first was the main port and capital, Lagos, where we arrived on January 11 1953.

Lagos is situated in a large lagoon, protected by long breakwaters, with a small quay adjacent to the city on one side, buoyed moorings in the middle and a line of more modern cargo berths on the opposite side, at Apapa.

At this time, Lagos still had mostly open sewers and you didn't have to walk far from the quay before you were in shanty-town. You soon got used to the pungent aroma and understood why it was that you could smell the place before you were even close enough to see it.

The weather was still hot and humid, although I was told that it became cooler at night ashore. I was more used to the heat of the day by now and sunburned shoulders had peeled and were beginning to turn brown. The unbearably itchy sweat rash had also subsided but nights on board were just as uncomfortable as ever. A system of piped fresh air pumped through the accommodation helped to ease the situation but the air was warm and had to be pointed directly at you to be even the least bit effective. Bed linen quickly became saturated with sweat and I was glad when the cargo was discharged about ten days later and we could set sail again.

The day after we left Lagos for Port Harcourt, I got the feeling that my shipmates were planning something so I was not totally surprised when the Fourth Mate, a passenger named Charlie who had befriended him and our two senior cadets produced a length of rope and, after a struggle, tied me to a chair and cut off most of my hair using lamp-trimming scissors. Admittedly, it had grown quite long by this stage of the voyage and apparently, I should have taken time off and used the services of a visiting barber in Lagos, which is what everyone else did.

Still, my ability to take this in good part earned respect, which was sadly not the case with the other junior apprentice; on his second trip, he became tearful when his turn came to undergo this treatment a few days later. Needless to say, I took time to have a proper crew-cut from a visiting barber at the next opportunity and stopped getting strange looks from the rest of the crew and the passengers. My hair has never been cut so short since.

Port Harcourt is an up-river port in the Niger Delta. After careful crossing of the sand bar at the mouth of the river, we were at a place called Bonny where we picked up, quite literally, a native pilot who was known to our Captain, complete with his family and their dugout canoe, using one of the ship's derricks. He guided us up various tributaries, through the African bush, and up to our destination, where we tied up to a small wharf and discharged the rest of our cargo. West Africa may not be a comfortable run to be on but it has to be one of the most fascinating.

After Port Harcourt, we went further southeast into the Bight of Biafra for brief stops at Douala in the French-controlled Cameroons and Victoria which is on an island off Equatorial Guinea, where we start loading small parcels of cargo - and, boy, was it hot.....

By the end of January, we were back at the Bonny Bar with the captain searching through his binoculars for the flag that our pilot would be flying over his dug-out canoe. Sure enough, he and his family were waiting for us as though they had been there since we put them back in the water about a week ago - but then, they probably had. Back at Port Harcourt, we started loading slings full of small, but extremely heavy, hessian bags of tin ore. As they were taken out of the sling in the bottom of the hold, dozens of huge cockroaches raced for cover. Whether their fascination lies in the tin or the hessian is a mystery. Whatever, no-one is likely to steal this cargo and that evening, the other junior apprentice and I took the opportunity to go ashore.

However, as dusk fell, we first had to negotiate our way along a wharf which was literally swarming with brown cockroaches, crunching them underfoot as we walked. I was able to get ashore again the following day when I was given time off by the First Mate, to compensate for working later than the others.

At this point in the voyage, the Chief Officer started to think about painting the ship, so that she would be in pristine condition when we finally arrived home and sailed up the Mersey. So, it was back to the soogee (washing with soda crystals) of all the paintwork, ready for repainting. The crew started hanging stages around the offshore side of the ship, out of the way of cargo work, in order to paint the black topsides down to the waterline. This would be continued in Lagos, our next stop, where we berthed three days later at Apapa Wharf.

We had arrived off Lagos before daybreak and whilst on anchor watch, I learned how to take bearings of the various light beacons ashore to check our position on the chart. This was always done, in case we dragged the anchor. It was less than 24 hours before we were on stations again for going into port. For this the Captain is of, course, on the bridge, with the Third Mate operating the engine room telegraph. In our case an apprentice, usually me, was charged with entering all the engine movements and the details of the transit and mooring in the ship's movement book. The more important details were added to the ship's log by a deck officer later.

The First Mate and an apprentice manned the forecastle, with the carpenter manning the windlass in case we needed to anchor in a hurry. As we neared our berth, this time at the Apapa Wharf, it was all hands to stations for mooring ship, with the Second Mate in charge aft. Before that, as we steamed towards the berth, the crew had raised all the derricks ready for a prompt start to loading.

It was in Apapa that we took on the bulk of our cargo and most of our passengers for the trip home. Our derricks were capable of lifting one-and-a-half tons at a time, but there were no small cranes or forklift trucks ashore, so each sling had to be loaded by hand, with native labourers carrying huge bags of palm kernels and groundnuts on their heads from inside the dock sheds.

The First Mate decided where each parcel of cargo was to be stowed so that the ship was always stable and so that it could eventually be discharged in the right order in the right port! Our main duty was now helping the officers to accurately stow the items, separate them with burlap and determine their position in the holds on a cargo plan. There were no company stevedores here.

Loading didn't take place on Sundays but we weren't complaining; the ship's cook took the opportunity to prepare a West African meal, usually a 'palm oil chop'. All the work and sea air meant I had developed a healthy appetite and, with some on board not too adventurous when it came to food, there was plenty for the rest of us; that day, I certainly left the table with a full stomach. The meal consisted of a bed of rice with a stew of meat, chicken and yams all cooked in palm oil, which was then liberally sprinkled with every kind of diced fruit and shredded nuts before more hot palm oil was added like gravy. After at least two helpings, this was followed by an afternoon siesta - it was heaven! There was even time to do some work on my somewhat-neglected correspondence course.

Although there were launches running across to Lagos during the day, we found that there was a seaman's club which had a swimming pool fairly close to the ship, on the Apapa side of the harbour. So, swimming trunks in hand, we decided to take the plunge. Then, we noticed the objects floating in the water which explained the unpleasant and pervading smell. We didn't bother to try to determine whether they had been left by an animal or a human and instead, we decided to give our swim a miss. Warnings that ears should be protected with plugs of cotton wool and Vaseline and that the water should not be swallowed seemed irrelevant.

February 9 saw us back at Freetown where we said goodbye to our Kroo Boys, who had given us such good service since they signed on just over a month ago. We apparently had enough fuel to get home and for the ship to move on to Las Palmas for the next voyage so we merely passed the Canary Islands, just before changing back into blue uniform ready for the fog and miserable weather we would meet as we got near home and the dreaded Irish Sea.

We would rendezvous with the Liverpool pilot vessel and pick up our River Mersey Pilot off Anglesea, in the lee of Point Linas. The shipping line, a Liverpool company, had their own contracted pilot who was ferried over to our ship in a small open cutter, crewed by two apprentice pilots.

They would carefully position him under the rope and wooden-slatted ladder which we had lowered over the ship's side. The trick was then for him to mount our ladder at the top of a wave and scramble up as quickly as he could before the next wave, which might have been bigger, lifted the boat up again to knock him off.

Having successfully reached the deck he then made his way up to the captain's cabin for a warming brandy or scotch whisky before appearing on the bridge where his local knowledge would be turned to good use as the ship made her way from the Mersey Bar light vessel up the buoyed channel and on to the welcome sight of the Liver Birds sitting atop the Royal Liver Building.

The Captain, or Master, who always retains the ultimate responsibility for the ship, even with a company pilot on the bridge, made sure his uniform cap was straight as we steamed up to an anchorage off the Liverpool waterfront, where we had to await boarding by immigration and port health officials. After their approval, we only had to wait for the tide. Finally the dock gates were opened and, after locking in to the dock system, we were able to make our way to the quay we had left two months earlier, before making the ship secure on her berth.

That night, I was home and in my own bed with a fund of stories to tell, although the trip was not officially over until all the officers and apprentices had been given their inward interviews at Head Office in the India Buildings and, more importantly, received their pay. In my case, thanks to a bill for my correspondence course, I discovered that I owed the company money!

I was given an advance of £5 to tide me over and instructed to work by the ship while the other apprentices had some leave. Then it was my turn, but it would only be just over a week before I was recalled to the same ship for my second voyage to West Africa.

# CHAPTER 4 - ALMOST AN OLD SALT

Three months into my apprenticeship, with one trip under my belt, I felt quite the old salt although, of course, I was still only the junior. We had only a few days working by the ship before we were due to depart on my second voyage and when we sailed, I was assigned to the 4-8 watch with our new First Mate or Chief Officer. If I thought my first voyage was hard, I was soon to learn that I had been given an easy ride.

I was on watch as soon as we left the Mersey and was exiled to the weather side of the bridge to keep a lookout, with the wheelhouse door firmly closed.

Brief trips across the wheelhouse to report seeing a ship or a buoy only made me feel even colder when I returned to my windswept vigil. Apart from the weather being wet and windy, the sea was quite rough and the ship was rolling heavily.

It was not easy on the stomach and the sole consolation of walking up and down the bridge wing was that one could time it so that you were always walking downhill! At 1800 hours, I was allowed in to make tea and have a 'smoko' even though I didn't smoke before it was back to my wet and windy post until 1945 hours when it was time to call the next watch with a hot cup of tea.

Our cabin was always warm and the joy of climbing into a warm bunk was only spoilt by being wakened again at 0345 hours so that I could pull on warm clothing again and report back to the bridge and the weather wing. At least it was starting to get light by the time I was called in to make the mid-watch cup of tea.

When I returned to the bridge, I was told to wear my dungarees and bring a bucket of water and a cloth with which to wash the wheelhouse windows, which were covered in salt spray.

The windows were like the old railway carriage windows, with a leather strap to pull them up. In order to clean them, I had to open one and sit outside, so that I could clean the windows on either side. By the time I had finished, my hands were like ice but at least we could see through the glass.

I was found other jobs to do until my watch was finished at 0800 hours, when it was back into uniform for breakfast in the saloon. I had already discovered that seasickness was an unwelcome friend which would come back to haunt me each time I had spent a period ashore and returned to bad weather, but the breakfasts would get better.

After breakfast and cabin cleaning, which was still my duty as junior apprentice, I was instructed to report to the bo's'n for work on deck with the crew, with the concession that I could knock off at 1530 hours in time for a shower - after all, I was due back on the bridge for the evening 4-8 watch!

This routine continued every day while we were at sea, except for Sundays when only the watch-keepers worked. As the weather and visibility improved, life on watch became more bearable and the Chief Officer would take time during the evening watch to instruct me in practical seamanship.

I was given stints on the wheel and I also had to learn how to box the compass - in other words, learn all the 32 compass points - as well as the not-so-practical things such as various rigs such as barques and brigantines. I also discovered that he knew our old neighbour, Captain Bill Andrews.

The Fourth Mate was also on the 4-8 watch and he introduced me to what is known as 'The Articles' or the Regulations for the Prevention of Collision at Sea. There are 32 and I was instructed to learn them word for word. As he was due to start college, ready to take his Second Mate's ticket at the end of this voyage, I suppose it was to his advantage as well as mine.

The 4-8 watch, of course, included both sunrise and sunset and both he and the First Mate would, whenever visibility was good enough, take sextant angles or 'sights' of the brighter stars in order to get a fix on the ship's position, leaving Yours Truly and the fo"c'sle lookout to watch out for ships.

We called at Las Palmas for bunkers before proceeding to West Africa, to visit more or less the same ports as on the last trip. Our longest stay was at Lagos in Nigeria, where we unloaded our deck cargo of quite large port launches, which required the crew to break out and operate our large jumbo derrick. This had a safe working load of about 50 tons and caused the ship to heel over slightly as the derrick swung over the side, before it came back upright as the weight came off again.

Homeward bound, we were also in Lagos for Good Friday and as we were loading by now, we had a day off. We took the opportunity to have a lifeboat drill and, having put our one motor-driven boat in the water, we loaded up with those crew and passengers who wanted to go and took a trip to the mouth of the harbour, round an inner breakwater and into Tarkwa Bay. This had a marvellous sandy beach and was, of course, the place from which our ship had got its name. It was also a favourite place of the ex-pats, including locally-based army personnel who even had a beach-side NAAFI where they could purchase food and drink at most reasonable prices.

Those of us who foolishly thought that we were used to the hot African sun were soon to be reminded that we were not. Swimming trunks are not the same as the shorts, socks and shoes that we wore aboard ship and all the bits that were normally covered became bright scarlet. This included the tops of our feet and even our shoulders, which had been kept relatively cool when swimming and which had been quite brown already, burned under the hot sun. By that evening, it was most uncomfortable, especially when having to wear our No 10 tunics and epaulettes for dinner in the saloon. Hundreds of tiny sweat blisters were to follow, but we all felt that a day like that was worth it.

We were again loading palm kernels and groundnuts, with the addition this time of hot palm oil, which was pumped into four deep tanks in one of the holds. If anyone was unlucky enough to fall in, there was little chance of getting them out and tales are told of finding nothing but the metal belt buckles of those unfortunates who did get too near to the edge of the tank and suffered the consequences. It was nice to know that you could end up in someone's tub of margarine!

I had realized that, apart from the Captain, I was the only 'officer' on the ship who was wearing old-fashioned and rather baggy uniform shorts so, before we left Lagos, I ordered a pair of trim, tighter-fitting, ones from one of the tailors who boarded regularly touting for business. Made to order, they were delivered the following day for the princely sum of fifteen shillings. I decided to acquire a more trendy shirt to go with them on my next voyage.

By the time we passed the Canary Islands again, on the way home, it was the end of April. The weather in the Irish Sea was much milder than when we sailed and, back in Liverpool, we signed off articles on May 8, my 17th birthday and the end of my second voyage to Africa.

Although the enthusiasm for travel and for my new career was undimmed, I had by now begun to think further ahead and was being influenced by the ship's officers talk of missed loved ones and their intention of 'swallowing the anchor' as soon as the opportunity arose. This seemed all too likely to explain the general demeanour of the ship's captains, most of whom seemed old enough to have survived both World Wars at sea, together with a severe world recession in between. Times were so bad then apparently, that many of them were reduced to sailing as ordinary seamen, even with captain's qualifications.

By now, I certainly had no intention of spending all my life at sea and certainly not of being confined to the Atlantic Ocean, although I would have no choice for the next four years if I were to fulfil my indentures. My plan for the future would be to complete my apprenticeship, qualify as a Second Mate and find a tramp-ship to take me anywhere but West Africa. After that, I wanted to qualify as First Mate and then join another liner company, perhaps going to New Zealand until I was 26 when I could finally qualify as a ship's Captain. By then, coincidentally, I would no longer be eligible for National Service, from which all seafarers were so far exempt. Then, I wanted to settle down to married life in a shore job, possibly in New Zealand.

# Chapter 5 - A Senior Apprentice Already

After just one week of leave I joined my next ship, the older MV Fulani, a sister ship to Bill Andrews's ship Fantee, which had been lost four years earlier on the Seven Stones Reef. Although this ship was rather elderly and therefore not as comfortable as the Tarkwa, I was the senior of just two apprentices and free at last from the chore of cabin-cleaning. We sailed a few days later, but were only on watches for three days before switching to day work. It would be a few more days before I got over my usual bout of seasickness, but I looked forward to reporting to the First Mate at 7am each morning to be given our jobs for the day.

*Voyage on SS Fulani to West Africa*

A brief call at Dakar in Senegal for bunkers, extended by half-a-day due to a minor engine problem, was our first port on this trip; apart from being another French colony, it had an island prison just offshore so there were shades of the Devil's Island and Monte Cristo in our minds.

Then it was on to the port of Monrovia in Liberia which is an interesting place in that, apart from having rubber plantations owned by the American Firestone Rubber Company, it is home to American Negroes who have decided to return to their roots.

We didn't see much of it, however; it was monsoon season and I had never seen such heavy rain. Just before leaving, we took on board some deportees, escorted by what looked like a black American policeman complete with guns, who we were to take to Freetown. There, we collected our Kroo Boys before continuing on the familiar round of West African ports, arriving at Takoradi Roads on May 30. We were tied up in the port, with the ship fully dressed in flags, for Coronation Day a few days later when we were able to go ashore and watch the local scout troops parading in celebration.

Life was much easier than on my last ship with the odd day off and time given for my correspondence course, thanks to the First Mate, Mr Hawkins. However, this was offset a

*Voyage on SS Fulani to West Africa. Dugout canoe*

little when my fellow apprentice, Jim Pearson, decided to get a touch of malaria; alas, that meant more work for me.

A couple more ports of call, places we had visited previously on the Tarkwa, then we were bound for Calabar, which is up another of the branches of the Niger delta in Nigeria.

We were to spend over a week loading and we began by filling our deep tanks with hot palm oil, which has to be kept hot in order to stop it solidifying. Back at sea, the movement of the oil when the ship rolled caused the tanks to sing through the expansion pipes like badly-tuned violins.

It was only a short sea trip to our next port of call, Victoria, which was quite spectacular. We anchored in what was described as an old volcano crater, with steep-sided islands all around us, dominated by the Cameroon mountains, whose higher summits are hidden in clouds and reach as high as 13,000 feet. We didn't get to enjoy the view for long, as there was a change of plan and we were soon on our way back to Lagos, arriving in the recently-vacated mailboat berth on Apapa Wharf on July 19.

So far, we had loaded the usual palm kernels and groundnuts but, four days later and shortly before sailing, we were to be faced with one of the more unusual deck cargoes to take on to Takoradi. The foredeck was cleared and filled with straw and a small herd of long-horned cattle assembled on the quayside.

I was fascinated to know how they were going to be lifted aboard, until someone lowered a hook to head height above the ground and the first four animals were hooked on, using ropes around the horns. As the wire was winched up, and after much bellowing and swinging of the horns, they were all lifted together, up and over the ship's rail and gently lowered to the deck. Then came the most dangerous part of the operation as they thrashed about, all trying to get back onto their feet. After a small stampede up the wharf, during which three animals actually disappeared (presumably having run straight off the end of the wharf and into the river), we managed to load just 97, complete with the herdsmen, who slept with them on deck for the sea passage to Takoradi.

*Loading Longhorn cattle on deck*

Trying to reach the fo'ç'sle from the bridge became a nightmare as the foredeck became a slippery mass of straw and very runny cow manure. The herdsmen and crew were kept busy lifting the poor animals back on their feet as the ship rolled in the swell and they slipped and spreadeagled. The first day of our ten-day stop at Takoradi was spent unloading them and washing the decks, but the smell lingered until we were back at sea.

We also carried a number of large logs, which were floated alongside the ship in huge rafts and then lifted aboard with our derricks to be lowered down into the hold, where they were stowed using wires and pulleys or blocks to haul them into the wings until the spaces were full.

When the hatches were full and battened down, we loaded more on the decks either side and the crew lashed them down with steel wire and bottle screws to make sure that they wouldn't move when the ship rolled in heavy weather. We finished loading and finally left the African coast at the beginning of August for the voyage home, stopping briefly at Freetown to let our Kroo Boys ashore and then at Tenerife in the Canary Islands for bunkers.

Our friend Frisco and his men who boarded the Tarkwa at Las Palmas were in Gran Canaria, of course, but in Tenerife there was another vendor of extremely dirty postcards and more wholesome Spanish sherry to take home - he would have been memorable for his black face and mop of white hair alone, without his name being Jesus Christ!

There always seemed to be an air of euphoria once we left the Canary Islands - this was described on board as having 'the channels.' I suppose this was due to the next arrival being the English Channel - or, in our case, Avonmouth in the Severn Estuary. Some of the crew were sent on leave here, but the rest of us had to wait another week until we arrived back in Liverpool. Another voyage over and a proper pay-off which would have to go on clothes as I was rapidly growing out of my civvies after three months at sea.

# CHAPTER 6 - ONE VOYAGE - THREE SHIPS

After ten days, my longest leave so far, I was ordered to join the good ship David Livingstone, quite a small Explorer class steamship, which was built soon after the First World War and had very basic accommodation. Fortunately, it was just a short voyage, down from Liverpool to the breakers yard at Grays on the River Thames in Essex, but it was a trip that would be remembered for two things.

*The SS Cambray*

*The SS Eboe*

The first came when our pilot appeared to have misjudged the strength of the ebbing tide - I will never forget the look of terror on the face of the lone rigger at the end of the wooden jetty as the line tightened and Father Thames tried to sweep us back down the river, lifting the whole structure off the piles. The fo's'le crew had to throw the turns of the windlass drum end before the mooring rope went slack, allowing it to crash down again.

The second was the Red Ensign which we were flying at the stern. I took it down with the other flags as one of my final duties on board when we were finally tied up alongside. It was a rather battered and holed flag and I have kept it to this day.

I was not to go home straight away, however. Along with the Third Mate, I was immediately transferred to another ship in London Docks called the SS Cambray. Built in

Canada for convoy duties towards the end of the Second World War, she was shortly to sail for West Africa. This was just as well, considering how expensive everything seemed to be in London and how little money I had left from my last trip's pay.

Our first port of call this time was Dakar in Senegal for bunkers and then Bathurst in Gambia, where we started to discharge our cargo. Sixty years later, I still find it difficult to understand why people would want to spend a hard-earned holiday in such a place. Then it was back to the usual ports except for Kita, where I briefly saw a sea turtle alongside the ship before it dived.

When we got to Lagos, I found myself packing my trunk again to be transferred to yet another, but much newer and faster, ship. Once packed I decided that, as my last job on the ship, I would give the cabin a final clean. In hindsight, this was probably not a good idea. In my haste, I plunged the toilet brush clean through the bottom of the pan, releasing a stench which rapidly filled the accommodation.  It was a most unwelcome farewell present for my shipmates and I left a most unhappy First Mate and carpenter, who would have the job of arranging the repair.

The MV Eboe, only a year old, was built at Greenock ready for conversion, if needed, into an armed merchantman. This meant that, apart from being capable of travelling at over 20 knots, she was also strengthened to carry a large gun on the fo'c'sle and a cannon on the bridge wings. She had been scheduled for a four-year voyage, trading between West Africa and the United States.

I joined her on October 20 to find that I was relieving "Crab" Smith, who had been the senior apprentice on my first trip. A few days later, my father received notice of my transfer and was advised that his son, Midshipman George E Dickinson, would not be home for at least another six months. All I knew was that I was going to see America and things were indeed looking up.

The ship was loading cocoa beans for Philadelphia and left in a few days for Takoradi on the Gold Coast, where we took on the last few tons of cargo before stopping at Freetown to drop off our Kroo Boys and head for Dakar and bunkers. The next stop would be Norfolk, Virginia.

The Master of the ship was Captain Coughlan. Unlike the other Captains whom I had so far sailed under, he allowed the apprentices to purchase beer from the ship's bar. Like the rest of the crew, we were also given a small tot of rum with the daily palludrine tablet which was issued as  protection against malaria.

The indentures that my father had signed when I was apprenticed made the Master of the vessel my guardian, as I was still classed as a minor. Their quaint wording stated that the apprentice was not allowed to frequent alehouses, taverns or places of ill repute, other than on the Master's business. Most other company Captains took that to mean that we were not allowed strong drink or any other kind of loose living whilst signed on their ship. I was still only 16, but this restriction was later to seem most unfair when, as with half the apprentices in the company, I had reached the age of 18.

Like most of the vessels in the company, we carried just 12 passengers. This restriction enabled the ship to sail without a ship's doctor  (crew didn't count towards the numbers) so we had to make sure that we never got too seriously ill or injured. As noted previously, this seemed to date back to the slaving ships where the slaves were a valuable cargo, to be looked after.

Our accommodation, however, was better than that on the Tarkwa and luxurious compared to the other vessels I had sailed on, even though we were still sleeping three of us in a four-berth cabin when the rest of the crew had single berths. When there were no passengers on board, we were even allowed to use the table tennis table at the after end of the promenade deck. Although I was junior apprentice again, our cabin was so big, with a bathroom and even a small study, that two of us shared the cleaning duties which made it not so onerous a task.

In order to get to our berth in Newport News in Virginia, we had to steam through Hampton Roads and past a whole fleet of American warships, including two huge aircraft carriers. It is considered etiquette for merchant ships to dip the Ensign as a courtesy to friendly warships and for them to dip their Ensign in acknowledgement. It gave us simple amusement to see a white-uniformed American matelot sent racing aft from the bridge to preserve US Navy pride.

There was no disguising the fact that this was an important naval base and when I did get ashore that evening, the town was full of American sailors in uniform. Unfortunately for us, the British pound sterling had just been de-valued but the shipping line, showing unusual generosity, subsidised us in order that we could receive the old rate of $4 to the £ instead of $2.80 but still it did not go very far. It would cost me almost 2 weeks' pay just to go to the cinema and have a hamburger and a piece of apple pie afterwards. For the first time, we were supplied with a rented television - this was a godsend as, unlike in West Africa, the dockworkers always finished at 5pm and we found ourselves with long evenings to fill.

By the time we reached Baltimore in the State of Maryland, we had earned a few more dollars and decided that, as this was reputedly the home of burlesque, we would have to see a burlesque show. Along with the other two apprentices, we found our way into the centre of the town and, not knowing where to find a theatre, decided to ask a policeman. When he heard that we wanted to see a burlesque show he couldn't have been more obliging.

"The Gaiety Theatre is what you want, boys" he said, "the best show in town!" He started to give us directions and then looked at his watch before declaring "you're gonna be late, the show is due to start in five minutes."

Without further ado, he walked straight into the middle of six lanes of traffic, blowing his whistle and holding up his arm, led us to a vacant taxicab and told the driver to take us to the Gaiety. After seeing us into the cab, his final words were: "Don't pay any more than a dollar fifty, boys. Enjoy the show."

It was dark when we found our seats near the front. We were enjoying the show, along with a few dozen American Navy men who whooped and whistled every time there was anything slightly rude on stage, but when the lights went up at the interval, we looked round to see that half our own crew were behind us, including the officers!

After the show, we went in a bar where despite having assured the barman that we were 18, he declined to serve us with the words; "sorry, boys, it's 21 in this State". A rude burlesque show was obviously not considered, by the State of Maryland, as harmful to the young as a cold beer.

After Baltimore, we travelled all the way up the Chesapeake Bay and through the Chesapeake Delaware canal to Philadelphia in Pennsylvania, which is a much more interesting place. I went to Independence Hall, where the Charter of Independence is on display along with the Independence Bell, although I suppose I was just as impressed by the tame squirrels who kept all the tourists amused. Another port of call for us was the British Legion, which cost 50 cents to enter but where the good people provided us with free beer and potato chips (crisps, to us). We had a few more nights of American TV and then it was off down the River Delaware, into the Atlantic again and up to New York.

To see, for the first time, the Statue of Liberty appearing out of the morning mist and then the Manhattan skyline as we approached was a sight not to be forgotten. We berthed at Hoboken, on the opposite side of the Hudson River to Manhattan on November 25 after a short drydocking to check the ship's bottom. The following day was Thanksgiving, so we got a bus and travelled by tunnel under the river to get into Manhattan for the must-do walk up Broadway.

We passed all the theatres and walked up to the ice rink at the foot of the Rockefeller Centre building with its Radio City Music Hall. We went to the British Apprentices Club in New York, which seemed to be well used and was run by a kind lady who supplied us with free sandwiches, but nothing stronger than milk from the fridge to wash them down. I met another British apprentice named Dickinson who was serving on a Lamport and Holt vessel trading between North and South America - I was rather jealous to find that he was paid more than we were, while he also received pay for overtime, which we did for nothing. Added to this, his company gave him the same special exchange rate which was given to us, namely $4 to the £ in the States!

After we left the drydock, we moved from the Hudson around the bottom of Manhattan to a berth on Pier 33 in Brooklyn; this was on the other side of the East River but still close to Manhattan and Broadway, once you got to know the subway.

While there, senior apprentice Emmerson and I were given tickets for a radio quiz show being broadcast at the weekend. We wore our uniforms just in case there was a chance for us to take part and win some money. Our strategy, however, was to no avail, a fact made more galling by the simplicity of the questions which won the contestants huge prizes. We were also treated with suspicion on the subway, mainly because we both offered our seats to ladies who were obviously not used to this kind of consideration.

During our stay in New York, we went to see a film at the Radio City Music Hall, a huge and quite luxurious 6,000-seat theatre. The evening wasn't expensive when you considered that we were treated to a stage show first, complete with a 36-strong chorus line called the Rockettes. Another impressive thing about cities like New York and Philadelphia, considering that this was still 1952, was the convenience of dispensing machines and water fountains - they seemed to be everywhere.

Another eye-opener was the Automat restaurant - you found your chosen meal or snack behind glass, inserted a coin and the door opened for you to take it. As soon as the door was closed a replacement appeared, inserted from a kitchen at the back, ready for the next customer - we thought this was revolutionary.

Just before leaving, I received a letter from home which included the telephone number of a relative of my mother, who was living in New York with his Italian wife Marguerita. Harry had been in Italy during and after the war and had a gift for languages, which he had put to good use as a translator at the United Nations. I managed to get hold of him and we arranged to meet the following day, December 3, at his office.

I decided to wear uniform, thinking that I would be easier for him to spot, but the main advantage of that turned out to be the attention I got from personnel in the United Nations building, all wanting to help and direct me!

I had never met Harry, but he and his wife took me for a most enjoyable dinner. This had been altogether a most enjoyable first time in New York and I was already looking forward to coming back.

The following day, we sailed up past Long Island on our way to the Cape Cod Canal, passing through New England countryside that was reminiscent of home before arriving at Boston, Massachusetts.

We only spent a couple of uneventful days there before taking on our passengers and leaving Boston for the 2,000-mile passage due south to the bottom of the Caribbean, passing the pirate Henry Morgan's stronghold, Mona Island, on the way. We then went on to our anchorage at Point Fortin, Trinidad where we were to load drums of the lake asphalt as our last item of cargo for West Africa. We were only at anchor for two days with no opportunity to go ashore, but entertainment came from watching the local stevedores dropping drums from the hatch coming down the hold, then seeing them burst when they hit the bottom, sending gouts of bitumen across the floor.

This was not entirely wasted as it resulted in trapping hundreds of cockroaches by the time we started to unload a few weeks later. The day after we sailed, on December 16, I had completed one whole year of my indentures and welcomed the subsequent pay rise - I was now earning just £100 per year.

# CHAPTER 7 - NOT HOME YET

We were back in West Africa and discharging our cargo before Christmas, arriving in Takoradi just in time for the celebrations to start. It was here that the senior apprentice, Emmerson, was transferred to another of the company's ships and in return we welcomed his replacement, Blakelock. Apart from the fact that he was two weeks junior to me, I remembered Blakelock as being a fellow trainee during my month at the Aberdovey Outward Bound School.

Another day at sea and we were anchored off Accra in time to welcome 1954, along with about seven other ships. The blowing of ship's whistles at midnight must have kept half of the Gold Coast awake.

A game of football was arranged against another company ship and we won 3-2. This was one of the few times that we were ever to get ashore at Accra but the journey was more enjoyable than the game, as it involved boarding one of the surfboats used for cargo and being paddled to a small beach just inside a small breakwater, then being carried through the surf on the back of one of the native paddlers. This was not quite as grand as the Company Agent's large wooden chair, or what we called the "Mammy Chair" that could be lifted on deck by the ship's derricks when loading passengers.

Although the method of discharging seemed fairly primitive here, having to use a surfboat for each one-and-a-half ton sling of cargo, it was quite efficient and the holds seemed half-empty by the time we left, about nine days later. Our stops became much shorter and in three weeks' time, we had called at Lagos and were loading cargo for the States again and were back in Takoradi via Duala and Lome.

Both the latter were French possessions and therefore were expensive places, but there were lots of expat French people living there. They seemed to look upon Africa as their home and not just a place to earn money, an attitude which seemed more common with the Brits. From a cargo-working point of view, these ports were quite different, with Duala being very mechanised and Lome another surf port although different from Accra in having steam launches so that the boats were towed, instead of having to be paddled. The launches were open boats with a wood-fired boiler complete with tall funnel amidships and so were reminiscent of Humphrey Bogart's boat in the film The African Queen. These ports may have been a little more modern than Accra, but were certainly not as efficient.

After Takoradi, we visited another French port, Abidjan on the Ivory Coast. This is situated inside what had been an inland lagoon until a channel was blasted through, opening it up to the Gulf of Guinea. We managed an evening ashore and were most impressed with the quality of the shops (a testament to the French attitude towards their colonies) saw a film at exorbitant cost and returned, with empty pockets, to our ship.

We sailed the following day, bound for Monrovia where we picked up our passengers for America. After that, it was back to Freetown to drop off our Kroo Boys and pick up our last passenger, who was to be the special responsibility of the apprentices on the voyage back across the Atlantic. He didn't have a name, so we christened him Tommy Trouble.

He was a very young chimpanzee and was bound, according to the label on his box, for El Paso in Texas. We would visit him regularly through the day with food, but it would upset him when we had to leave him alone again to carry out our other duties.

From Freetown, we were set on a course direct to New York which meant that, a few days before arrival on February 16, we passed from the nice warm Gulf Stream directly into the Labrador Current. This was brought forcibly to our attention at about 3am when we all awoke and searched for extra blankets as the temperature suddenly dropped by about 30 degrees. It was only later that we remembered poor Tommy in his box, down in the shelter deck baggage room and after we managed to thaw him out, he spent the rest of the trip in our cabin, being thoroughly spoilt.

He was, apparently, only about two months old and all he wanted to do on first being let out of his box was to cling to you like a small child; then he would offer a finger to your mouth, perhaps as a sign of submission or, it seemed, affection before gratefully taking and peeling a banana. We got quite fond of him, despite having to pick up all the skins and I often wondered after he carried on his journey to El Paso whether that was just a staging point on his way into orbit, as the US space programme was already underway. We used to let him out for a stretch and exercise and never had any trouble getting him back in his box - but he must have learned how to open the door.

He escaped on the day we started cargo work at our berth on Staten Island and you would have thought he was a gorilla the way the dockworkers scattered in panic, even though they were all twice his size. We eventually caught him and later that day, we said 'goodbye'. Our consolation on losing him was the $5 each we received as our share of the $25 bonus paid by the shippers for looking after him.

I had also saved a little more money this time and, determined to make the most of my time in the US, took another trip to the Rockefeller Centre Building. Even though it was not quite as high as the Empire State Building, you could still see the whole of Manhattan, from Yonkers at the top end to Central Park and the Battery at the bottom. The day was rounded off with another show at the Radio City Music Hall, complete with the premier of "The Long, Long Trailer" which was introduced in person by the stars of the film, Lucille Ball and her husband Desi Arnez.

Having the weekend off, I had arranged to go and visit Harry Burroughs and his wife so I left the ship straight after lunch on Saturday, taking a bus to catch the Staten Island Ferry across to Manhattan and the subway up to Grand Central Station. This looked more like a huge marble-tiled cathedral than a railway terminus, with a bar serving coffee and hamburgers instead of an altar, until you passed through one of the doors and found yourself on a railway platform.

Harry and his wife Marguerita lived in a place called Bronxville which was a way out of Manhattan following the River Hudson. I was met by Harry who walked me through some very pleasant suburbs before we got to their flat where Marguerita was preparing dinner. After dinner, another English colleague of Harry's arrived with his Scandinavian wife and we sat drinking and talking until late.

I was easily persuaded to stay the night, sleeping on a bed-settee which, I have to say, was much more comfortable than the bunks I had now got used to. I returned to my ship the following day but, as the next day was Monday and the anniversary of George Washington's birthday, I had yet another day off. Therefore, I met them at Grand Central Station in time to bring them back to my ship where I had arranged for them to have dinner. They met my cabinmates Ross and Blaiklock and we had a few drinks before I took them back to the Ferry Terminal on their way back to Manhattan. They seemed impressed with our ship and

I think they enjoyed the day. My shipmates were certainly smitten by Marguerita.

Another faint relation of mine, this time on my father's side of the family, lived in Connecticut. He had been in touch with us suggesting that I might like to visit on my next trip to New York and I sensed that seeing someone from home might be giving as much pleasure to these comparative strangers as their welcome was giving me. I had already decided to request another States trip before being transferred again to go home and hoped to be back soon.

Whilst the berth in Staten Island was rather a long way from Manhattan, we had discovered what the Americans call a "diner' quite close to our berth where we could enjoy a huge slice of apple pie under an inch-thick layer of cream, together with coffee, for only 30 cents. We even got a nice smile from the waitress and the whole thing seemed a real bargain even then.

Baltimore was our first brief stop for loading and then it was on to berth at a place called Paulsborough on the River Delaware before returning to good old Pier 33 in Brooklyn to finish cargo work, take on passengers and hand back the rented television, which had kept us up far too late at night watching old films.

Just before we sailed, on March 10, we found out that, after loading in West Africa, the Eboe would now be returning home to England and not returning to the United States. I called both Harry and Mrs Dickson in Connecticut to give them the news and told them I hoped to see them when I next got the chance to visit the US.

About ten days later and just 60 miles off Freetown, we saw a small rowing boat which appeared to be in distress and so we hove to. The African fishermen on board had run out of drinking water and, after replenishing their water containers, they refused a lift back into Freetown in order to carry on fishing - but it did seem to us a long way offshore for a rowing boat. Complete with Kroo Boys, we then called at Monrovia to let off our passengers before proceeding directly to the River Congo and my first crossing of the Equator. For better or worse, Father Neptune was not to come aboard and I never made his acquaintance.

The place we were bound for was over 100 miles up the river, in what was known as the Belgian Congo, where once again French was spoken by both the whites and the blacks. This was quite different to the River Niger; it was very hot but with pleasant country and rolling hills on either side, although navigation in a large ship still had its moments. The most impressive came just before we arrived at Matadi, our destination, when we turned a corner into what was known as "The Devil's Cauldron." The strong current coming downstream, through a fairly narrow channel, caused a whirlpool which we had to negotiate before entering a wider stretch again leading up to our berth.

Like other French-speaking colonies, life seemed more civilised and whilst in Matadi, we were able to visit the local swimming pool to cool down. Fortunately, we had shipmates who knew their way around so language was not so much of a problem and, just four days later, we were on our way back through the Cauldron and back down to the sea.

Lagos, Accra and Takoradi followed, where we completed discharge and then another trip up the less appealing River Niger to Calabar for palm oil, followed by a different tributary to reach Port Harcourt and then back to Lagos to finish loading for home. Ever since we started loading, all hands (including the Kroo Boys when at sea) had to work frantically to clean and paint the ship ready for when we were due to arrive back in the River Mersey. Even so, we got a long weekend off in Lagos including Monday when, having put down the motor lifeboat as part of one of our regular drills, the Master allowed one of the officers to take us to Tarkwa Bay, just inside the western breakwater at the entrance to Lagos harbour.

The beautiful sandy beach was full of day-trippers enjoying the sun. This really was a popular place for the Europeans working in Lagos, particularly the Army personnel with their families. The beach NAAFI was open and we were able to purchase egg & chips and a bottle of locally-brewed Star lager.

A few days later, the Managing Director of the shipping line arrived and our Captain, who had been expecting a visit, gave orders that all the accommodation should be given an extra clean. An apprentice had to keep watch all afternoon at the top of the gangway and call the Captain in time for him to arrive, complete with uniform cap on, to salute the MD. We finally left Lagos on April 21, bound for Freetown where we dropped our Kroo Boys and loaded bananas on deck, only calling at Las Palmas after that for bunkers and just 200 tons of tomatoes, arriving back in Liverpool on May 6, just 2 days before my 18th birthday.

# CHAPTER 8 - MY FIRST "UNCLE" SAM BOAT

After eight-and-a-half months away from home, my leave this time was just under three weeks before I joined my next ship, the steamship Zini, in London docks, along with my cabin-mate from the Eboe, Joe Ross. Built in America for convoy duties during the War, this was the first of three liberty ships, as they were called, on which I sailed. Although they had a poor reputation in the British Merchant Navy, I could never see why.

More popularly known as "Sam Boats" they were built at great speed on the basis that they may not survive more than one Atlantic crossing and were, it was true, rather utilitarian. However, for the ship's crew, they were very practical. All the accommodation was in one block amidships, so no-one had to venture out on to the deck in bad weather, either to get to the galley, go down to the engine room or go up to the bridge, or indeed man the lifeboats should the need arise.

Freetown was our third port on this voyage and we had the pleasure of berthing at the brand new wharf, where we unloaded some fine English motor cars, including Austins and Hillmans, from the 'tween-deck cargo spaces. We enjoyed this particularly as the apprentices got to steer them as they were pushed into position under the open hatch by the dock workers, ready for lifting out. Being under a ton-and-a-half in weight, this could be done using the normal wires and derricks which we used for the usual slings of cargo. Whilst here, a number of the crew including the First Mate and the Bo's'n revealed themselves as keen fishermen, causing some ribbing by casting their lines over the side. A 3-feet long Red Snapper silenced any banter from the rest of us when it was landed on the deck.

Complete with our complement of Kroo Boys, our next port of call was Takoradi, prior to arriving in Accra where we discharged cement from all hatches for almost a fortnight before leaving there for Keta and then the Apapa wharf at Lagos. The poor crews of the surf boats would have to slip over the side and wash off the cement dust before starting the long paddle back to the shore.

July and August is the rainy season in West Africa. This brings with it slightly cooler temperatures, particularly at night. Therefore, sleep on board was much easier although, apart from the surf ports, the working day was from 7am until 7pm or even 11pm when we were behind schedule. This meant there was little time for pleasure, or my correspondence course, for that matter. Being at anchor in all the surf ports, the apprentices are used for keeping watch through the night. This involved taking regular compass bearings of the lights ashore to make sure that the anchor was not dragging. Sleeping during the day when cargo was being worked was not easy, although there was some compensation in the midnight feast of bread and sausage or bacon which had been left out, together with whatever food we could sneak from the cook's stores!

Arrival off Lagos found us without a berth, another vessel having been given priority, so we had to swing at anchor for almost a week before taking our pilot on August 7. By now, I was getting quite attached to anchor watches and my egg and bacon sandwich at midnight.

After Lagos, we headed for the Bonny bar and the Niger Delta, to find that we were rationed to fresh water; the tanks had been pumped out in order to scrape over the sandbar without losing any of the precious cargo destined for Burutu and Warri. Conditions for the crew were never the priority where cargo was concerned.

After discharge was complete, we headed further up the delta to Sapele to start loading a full cargo of timber for South Africa. Steaming through the African bush seemed an adventure in itself, with the odd sighting of a crocodile, actual or imaginary, and small riverside settlements with the early risers, as it always seemed to be just after dawn, blearily watching us pass by as they attended to their bodily functions from a tree overhanging the water. On the few occasions when we were to pass later in the day, the canoes would swarm out filled with native children calling out "Dash me, Joe" to the crew, enjoying the experience without, it seemed, any real expectation.

One other point of interest was "the Bend" where we had to enter one tributary, well into the delta, from another, involving a turn of 90 degrees. This was achieved by approaching at slow speed and then ringing full ahead on the ship's telegraph whilst at the same time going hard-a-port into the river's flow.

This manoeuvre was sometimes successful; more often, it failed and the First Mate and the carpenter on the fo'ç'sle would disappear briefly into the trees until engines were put astern and that, together with the river flow, would carry us back in midstream and heading in the right direction. This was enough to give any captain who was not used to West Africa a heart attack, but the deep gouges all along the mudbank showed that we were not the first vessel to round "the Bend" in this way.

Arrival at the delta ports was always something of a disappointment, as they were hardly ever more than a riverside wharf backed by a small shanty town. The one exception seemed to be Sapele, which had no proper wharf but did have a sawmill, backed by a small shanty town.

Prior to arrival we had to unship our kedge anchor, which was housed against the small poop house aft. It had to be lifted using one of the after-derricks and hung over the starboard side, attached to the heaviest mooring or towing wire we had. On arrival at our berth, both this and the starboard bow anchor were dropped and mooring lines were taken ashore on the opposite bank of the river using launches. After that, we had to lower out more and more rope, which disappeared into the bush until it looked as though we were going to have to run out and fetch it. Eventually, the cry came to heave away and, with some relief, the lines were passed around the windlass on winch.

Water-soaked rope began to pile up again on deck. It was only after distant branches started to shake that we realised that our 7,000-gross ton ship was being moored to trees! It was then a case of adjusting our position using anchor cable, wire and mooring ropes, ready to start loading from both sides of the vessel. This we did lifting planks of sawn timber in loose slings from barges, which were then stowed one by one, as though we were laying deck upon deck. At other holds, we were picking up huge logs from floating rafts, which I had already had experience of stowing deep in the holds using steel blocks and wires. These rafts had come down river with the more dense hardwood logs, known as sinkers, being supported by the less dense timbers.

A few days later, after working cargo day and night, we left Sapele to finish loading more sawn timber and logs at Lagos and then another 3,000 tons at Takoradi. This would take us 18 days thanks to a labour dispute, but completed our full capacity of 10,000 tons. We sailed, bound for Cape Town, where we would arrive twelve days later, on September 24 1954. As we steamed south at our average speed of around 10 knots the Bo's'un, who was, without doubt, our keenest fisherman, trailed lines astern which were continually being lost until eventually, in desperation, he trailed some eighth-inch steel wire, sprung at the ship's side, with a home-made lure and a seven-inch hook. When this was also lost, we were already approaching the Cape so further attempts to hook a sea monster would have to wait.

The backdrop of Table Mountain appeared on the horizon long before we could actually see Cape Town but once we had picked up the pilot, it didn't take long before we were in the shelter of the long breakwater protecting the harbour from the southern ocean. I knew that one of my old Scout Masters from Ormskirk, John Blundell, had emigrated to Cape Town and soon after we tied up, a telephone was placed on board complete with a Cape Town telephone directory. There were only three Blundells listed and, as luck would have it, his was the first name I tried.

His family had actually donated our headquarters in Ormskirk soon after the first World War. He had emigrated to South Africa a few years before and my call, out of the blue, must have surprised him, but he immediately arranged to come down to the ship and pick me up the following day, a Sunday.

A few of us had planned to go up Table Mountain that day but sadly, strong winds meant that the cable cars were not running and as we were due to sail again on Monday, the opportunity was lost. However, the view alone from our berth was worth our being here. It is also, apparently, common for mist to creep over the top and roll down  during the late afternoons, until the mountain and part of Cape Town itself are enveloped.

My trip with John Blundell and his wife was to take us about 60 miles inland, through mountain passes and along some exceedingly rough road, but the scenery was wonderful. We visited some gardens with the most exotic wild flowers and a native village which must have been a regular tourist spot as we were shown inside the small houses, which were made of what seemed like straw. I was entertained to dinner at his house, located on the side of a hill overlooking Camps Bay which had the most wonderful view, before he and his wife brought me back to the ship. Even that short journey meant driving over a hill called the Lion's Head, from which the night-time view of Cape Town, with the harbour lights spread out below, was an imposing sight.

Leaving Cape Town, we rounded the Cape of Good Hope and arrived in Port Elizabeth two or three days later. I'm sure it's a nice place but I'm afraid it wasn't memorable. We sailed again just a couple of days later.

East London was our next port of call and although it was not so impressive from a scenic point of view, it was what you may call seaman-friendly. This was mainly due to the padre at the Seaman's Mission who, having persuaded the first mate to give us time off on Sunday, recruited half-a-dozen of us to go to his church. This was not so much of a chore as he organised a picnic in the afternoon with lots of female company.

In fact, he organised dances at the mission almost every other night and there were always plenty of local girls attending. It was said that many of them end up marrying seafarers but whether that was the reason for the popularity of these events, or the sight of the padre with a cigarette in his mouth and playing the drums for all he was worth is anybody's guess. He also managed to arrange a football match where we had the satisfaction of beating the crew of a Norwegian ship 5-0.

Like most port Padres, he was a generous and good-hearted man who remains my firmest memory of East London, despite the evening that our very large Welsh Fourth Engineer, who claimed to be an ex-boxer and was normally a quiet chap, arrived back on board drunk and in fighting mood. He appeared to take exception to laughter heard in the cabin I was in, assuming it was directed at him. I was with my fellow apprentice, the Purser and another junior engineer and he assaulted all four of us. Ten minutes later, he came back and apologised but the side of my face was sore for a couple of days.

October 8 found us in Durban where we would complete discharge of our cargo and start loading general cargo to take back to West Africa. Whilst not as spectacular as Cape Town, Durban appeared quite an elegant city with a waterfront of tall white buildings. With South Africa still under apartheid, it had been made very clear to us that undue fraternising with non-whites was a criminal offence, but it did come as something of a surprise that they also had a Victorian outlook when it came to swimming attire.

On the Sunday, when there was no cargo work, we decided to go to the beach and found that there were purpose-built changing rooms which you could use for a small charge. However, on trying to exit the place wearing my smart, if slightly small, laced-up swimming trunks, I was stopped by the attendant. He warned me that unless I was better covered I was in danger of being arrested.

I then spent the day wearing a larger, hired pair with the letters DC, presumably standing for Durban Council, in large print across the front. Mindful of the frequent sightings of sharks on this coast, it was a relief to see the shark net surrounding our stretch of the beach and we were careful to stay within it.

Eight days later, we sailed for Cape Town, with an extra 2,000 tons of cargo for discharge there before resuming loading our cargo for the West African coast and another chance to see John Blundell and his wife. This time, we had lunch at his house before driving to a lovely and obviously popular beach at a place called Llandudno. Like its North Wales namesake, it had a Great Orme rising behind it with the addition of some picturesque rock formations and caves.

This was followed by dinner and drinks back at his house and a trip to the cinema. They were then kind enough to run me back to the ship, on the way stopping at the first drive-in diner I had ever seen, despite my earlier visits to America.

We managed to play a couple of football matches before sailing. One was against a team partly made up of the crew from a small European tug on its way for delivery in Australia. The heavy seas around the Cape seem too big for such a small vessel and two of the crew jumped ship before they sailed.

I don't know whether the strong winds here on our first visit had damaged the cable car, but it was out of action and under repair whilst we were in Cape Town this time so, sadly, I never did get the chance to go up Table Mountain.

On our way back up the coast, we were accompanied by schools of porpoise. There seemed to be hundreds of them, up to eight feet in length and leaping out of the water so close alongside that you could clearly see the small air-holes in their backs. The Bo's'un had had his wire fishing line out again but whatever took the bait one night broke the wire again.

Before we arrived, on October 30,, at our final loading port on the edge of the Namibian desert, we heard the sad news that the small tug with whose crew we had played football at the Cape had disappeared and was presumed lost with all hands. The two deserters must have had a premonition, or finer judgment of the situation than their shipmates.

Walvis Bay was a whaling and fishing port and mainly German-speaking, except for a sizable number of ex-pat Scotsmen who worked in the large fish-canning factory there. We were due to load a mere 500 tons of dried and tinned fish and, because our crew had proved troublesome when in drink after signing on in London, the Captain decreed that there was to be no shore leave here and no issue of money, in an attempt to prevent any delays to the ship's schedule. All ratings had already had their tap stopped, which meant no access to the supply of alcoholic drink on board.

As we were casting off the mooring lines during the afternoon of the following day, the last two Able Seamen of those who had sneaked ashore the previous night came running up the jetty and were pulled on board, to be logged the next morning and fined by the Captain. When I asked one of them how they still managed to get drunk with no money to spend, I was gleefully reminded that a Scotsman didn't need money once he had found the Scottish Club in a place like Walvis Bay.

The desert was so flat and the whole place so low-lying that, soon after sailing, it had disappeared from view astern.

The men from Stornoway were fine seamen and most were very likable when sober, but some of them hadn't been back home for over 20 years and, on paying off a ship, would spend all their money on drink and loose women in the port of London before signing on again. Their poor behaviour record would ensure that this was most likely to be an old tramp ship. The two who were almost left in Walvis Bay were obvious alcoholics and I was to witness what I was to learn later to be delirium tremens or DTs, as one of them would try to fight off the demons which he imagined were attacking him.

For the second time on this trip, we were to sail up the river Congo to Matadi. We arrived there on Guy Fawkes Day, to share the jetty with another British ship. The apprentices had been to the same pre-sea school as my cabin-mate and we felt a little more fortunate to learn that their voyages averaged 18 to 24 months!

As we were now both quite experienced, we were being given a wider and more interesting range of jobs to do on board, from taking spells at the wheel to working aloft at sea and, whilst in port, spending more time in uniform assisting the officers rather than just cargo-watching. A Danish ship arrived before we left a few days later and we managed to get in another game of football, winning 8-0 which made up for their vessel being much more modern than ours!

We were back in Lagos, after another quick trip up "The Creeks" , as we called the Niger delta, by the time we learned that we were to load for home this time with, possibly, a few of the continental ports on the way. Unfortunately, sawn timber was likely to be a large part of our cargo, so there was no chance of being home for Christmas.

The end of February was a more likely timescale, but at least we were to head in the right direction. Before leaving Lagos, we were surprised one day to see a water-skier shooting past the ship and on down the harbour. This was not something I had seen before, as it was hardly a popular pastime in 1953 and it was certainly a most unusual sight in West Africa.

It took us some time to complete discharging before we could start to prepare the holds for our homeward cargo of timber and start loading, as we seemed to visit every port on the West African coast (and some twice) in the process.

Apart from the fore peak store being broken into and our stock of paint stolen (suspected to be the work of our crew looking to trade it for hard liquor), nothing of note happened except for success for our fishermen in Takoradi. We were loading cargo at the buoys and, following a lunch break spent diving off the ship's side and doing backward somersaults into the water off the logs floating near the foot of the gangway, the Second Mate caught a 42lb snapper, followed soon after by the Bo's'un catching a huge ray with a tail that lashed around the deck until the carpenter managed to chop it off with an axe. Needless to say, there were no more swimmers for the rest of our stay.

Christmas was spent at sea after leaving Abonema, which still seemed to rely on oil lamps for lighting and where we had loaded palm oil in our deep tanks. Those who were not on watch, and perhaps some that were, all got extremely merry and there were a lot of sore heads, including mine, as we went on stations at 6am for arrival in Lagos. Being up so early left me tired but reasonably clear-headed, unlike my cabin-mate who could not be roused and descended into hangover hell as the day progressed.

After lunch, the port health launch called at all the ships offering a trip to Tarkwa Bay beach and I was one of the few to take advantage. On Boxing Day, which was not classed as a holiday on board ship, my fellow apprentice had recovered and we were both turned to painting the ship's hull whilst there was no cargo work. Ross and I had the job of painting in the ship's draught marks at stem and stern, whilst hanging off in a bo's'un's chair, a big change from swimming off a tropical beach!.

Three days later, we left for Takoradi and then called at Freetown for a day before bunkering at Dakar. In the event, we had not loaded any sawn timber and the ship was full of logs with some palm kernels and bales of cotton and rubber in the tween decks. We were now well into 1955 and the Bay of Biscay was living up to its reputation, with rough seas and poor visibility. We picked up the pilot at the mouth of the river Maas just after midnight and by noon on January 24, we were on our berth at Rotterdam. The feeling of euphoria had not been dampened by having to do double-watches, which meant four hours on and four hours off for several days due to having to navigate the English Channel, one of the busiest stretches of water in the world and particularly difficult in the winter weather. At last, we could catch up on some sleep.

A modern berth allowed all the Rotterdam cargo to be discharged in double-quick time and we had steamed up the river Elbe and were in Hamburg by the end of January. Our berth was on the opposite side of the river to the city and when we finally managed to get ashore to do some last-minute souvenir shopping, it entailed catching a ferry which seemed reasonably priced at 15 pfennigs each. Not wishing to risk not have enough money for the return fare, I carefully counted out a reserve of another 30 pfennigs before we went any further. We had a pleasant time that afternoon sightseeing, not missing the famous "Winkelstrasse" with the sign at both ends indicating that it was barred to all Allied personnel. As neither of us had any money left, there was no way that we could afford the wares that were on offer in each shop window!

Eventually, we arrived back at the ferry, only to have our request for tickets refused as the price apparently went up at night. Fortunately, there was a German dock worker behind us in the queue who saw our predicament and insisted on paying our fares. He even refused my proffered 30 pfennigs, proving that Germans weren't all bad. On coming out of drydock, the ship was ballasted but still high out of the water as we sailed for the Thames and London.

Crossing the North Sea, the weather was so bad that at times we were making no headway at all and I have never forgotten the tiny trawlers that we passed, with the fishermen, clearly seen in our binoculars, as they hung over the side, in heavy seas and icy water, pulling their nets in by hand. Those men certainly earned their living and I thought of them for years afterwards, every time I visited a chip shop. We finally tied up at our berth in the London docks and were paid off on February 8. Inspection of the crew's quarters soon after revealed bare cabins, some of our Stornoway friends having apparently sold or exchanged everything, including their bedding, whilst in Hamburg for the money to buy more drink. They may have suffered for it whilst crossing the North Sea or perhaps they were too drunk to feel the cold! I drew some money for the train journey to Liverpool and home, after a voyage to South Africa and back which had taken more than eight months.

# Chapter 9 - My First Stowaway

During another non-too-generous three-week leave period, I bought my first sextant. I got it from an ex-River Yangtse pilot who had been a prisoner of war in the Far East. It was a small yacht sextant made by Heath & Co of London and it cost me just £10.

*MV Swedru*

I then received orders to join my next ship, which was not quite as new as the Eboe and certainly not as fast. The Swedru had a Doxford diesel engine with just four cylinders instead of six and a modest cruising speed of about 13 knots, which was still much better than the 10 knots of the steamship Zini. The weather was still cold and wet and I was glad to sail after a week working by as loading was completed.

When we arrived in Dakar for bunkers, it was to discover that about ten of the crew, including yours truly, needed vaccinations; we obviously all welcomed the opportunity of a run ashore, no matter what the reason.

We were taken to a local hospital in three taxis, all driven by French-speaking Africans wearing a kind of burnoose together with a red fez. When one of the other drivers passed us, it rapidly became something of a race with the passengers shouting encouragement as we hurtled along with complete disregard for other traffic on the road.

Our driver kicked off his sandals in an effort to press the accelerator closer to the floor but, sadly, we still came second. A memorable four hours after arriving, we were heading away from Dakar and to our first port for discharge.

Whist at sea, I was getting the opportunity to practice taking altitudes of the sun with my own sextant. About twice a week, under the supervision of the Second Mate who was officially the ship's navigating officer, I would take a sight before breakfast when the sun was rising in the east. Coupled with an exact time by the ship's chronometer, this gave an approximate longitude.

Another altitude taken at noon, with the help of the other officers including the Captain, would give us a latitude and an observed position at midday.

The Swedru, like most of the more modern company ships, carried 12 passengers and had a table tennis table at the aft and sheltered end of the passenger deck which, sadly we were not allowed to use. In fact, the passengers hardly used it, either. Their evenings were spent, by the ladies at least, watching the Kroo Boys carrying out their ablutions after a hard day's work. This consisted of them stripping naked and using a bucket of warm water obtained from the crew pantry to have an overall wash - I suppose it was equivalent to an early version of the Chippendales.

When we arrived at Lagos on March 24, the last of our passengers left the ship and the table tennis table was finally ours, at least for a few weeks. All the cargo berths were full and almost all the officers, apart from the Captain who rarely if ever mixed socially, would congregate at the after end of the passenger deck for endless competitions mixed with the inevitable cold beer, gin and tonic or in our case, a soft drink!!

Our itinerary was made known at last and we discovered that we were to be loading for Newfoundland and America, so it was to be another long trip. My cabin-mate on this voyage, Jim Pierce, was an ex-HMS Conway cadet and although junior to me, he had a year's remission so that we would be up at college for our Second Mate's exams at about the same time. We were having more free time so far on this voyage and I was up to date with my correspondence course.

We were delayed in Accra for a few weeks by storms and very heavy monsoon-type rain which prevented cargo work, so we had even more time for table tennis. This was particularly true as, being anchored almost a mile out, there was no opportunity to go ashore.

Eventually, we got down to our last table-tennis ball, as wild shots would send the ball flying over the ship's side or down the after deck where it would find a scupper before a frantic chase could catch it. Eventually, we got quite good at shinning down a guy-rope, fishing the ball out of the water as it floated past on the current, popping it into our mouths and climbing up again to play another game. In those days, nobody had heard of Health & Safety.

Eventually, fully loaded with cargo but no passengers, we left Dakar, our last port in West Africa, for Newfoundland. It was May 6, just two days before my 19th birthday and three days before I would sit my second-year correspondence-course examinations. Just under a fortnight later, we left the warm Gulf Stream and crossed into the Labrador Current and found ourselves in icy cold fog, hearing weather reports warning of icebergs.

The sea was quite smooth and, being a fairly modern ship, we had radar so when the icebergs showed up on the screen, it was easy to alter course to avoid them. Disappointingly, the same fog prevented us from actually seeing an iceberg but the air temperature as we passed was proof enough that they were there. It came as a surprise to note that we were on a latitude just a few degrees south of Liverpool, which showed the difference that ocean currents can make to the weather conditions.

The port of St John's was accessed through a narrow gap in a shoreline of steep cliffs and, in the persistent fog, even our radar failed to show the entrance until we were quite close.

We then had to push our way through small floating ice floes, with steep cliffs close on either side, before the harbour opened up before us. As well as a number of cargo ships, we found the harbour full of fishing boats and were surprised to see that many of them were flying the Portuguese flag. Apparently, the Portuguese fished these waters as the British fleets fished those off Iceland, but a snug harbour was obviously the place to be in such foggy conditions. Even Gander Airport had been shut down, which meant no mail from home until we sailed again a few days later for the much warmer temperatures of Virginia and Maryland.

The weather there was glorious and as we travelled through the rivers and sheltered waterways, everywhere we looked there were motor cruisers and yachts on the water - even through the length of the Chesapeake and Delaware Canal en route to the port of Philadelphia. Eventually, on June 3, we arrived in New York and received our first mail from home since leaving West Africa.

I had written to Mrs Dickson from St John's before we left, with an approximate ETA for New York but it was still a surprise, on our first morning at pier 33 in Brooklyn, to be relieved from tallying bags of cocoa on the foredeck by the First Mate who told me that I was wanted on the telephone.

It was even more of a surprise to be met by our Captain and be told that I was being given the weekend off, before being handed the telephone. I found that I was speaking to a Mr John Bennet, the adopted son of Mrs Dickson, who arranged to meet me in the Staten Island Ferry car park later that day. I quickly packed a few things and caught the subway into Manhattan and down to the ferry landings at the Battery, in time to catch the 12 o'clock ferry.

He was easy to spot, being in a huge (by British standards) white Cadillac. After we had introduced ourselves, he told me that he ran a marine engineering supply company in New York which had been started by his adoptive father, Stewart Dickson. He had telephoned, apparently, from his friend Mr Ealand's office. Mr Ealand just happened to be the manager of Booth American Lines, our agents in New York, which explained a lot about my sudden weekend leave. He had a business meeting later that day and was unable to take me himself but suggested that we had some lunch, after which he would return me to the ferry with instructions on how and where to catch a bus to Mrs Dickson's hometown of Ridgefield in Connecticut.

For lunch, we drove to the Staten Island Country Club, which would be described to me by New Yorkers as being harder to get into than Heaven. When we arrived, I could understand why.

Apart from being a very good golf club, we passed tennis courts and a large swimming pool as we approached the clubhouse, where an attendant was given the keys in order to park the car. We had a drink and sat at a table to study the menu which seemed spartan compared to the surroundings in that all I could see were sandwiches. Another gentleman joined us, a friend of John Bennet's, who was introduced as a judge.

We all ordered a turkey sandwich. When it arrived, it certainly consisted of bread and slices of turkey but was like no sandwich I had seen before. The plate was filled and was complete with French fries and salad, together with a generous covering of gravy.

I finished it way behind my companions and barely had time for ice cream before we were all three in the Cadillac and racing to catch the ferry back to Manhattan. The Judge, I was to learn later from Mrs Dickson, had been provided with the financial backing he needed to become elected to office by her husband Stewart. The American justice system appeared quite different to ours.

For 10 cents, the Staten Island ferry was one of the best sightseeing bargains in New

York. Yet I was more concerned in getting up to Manhattan and catching my bus than taking in the scenery; fortunately, I was just in time. Although the Arrow Line bus was ultimately bound for Boston, my journey would only take me about 60 miles and the driver kindly told me when we arrived at my stop. There was no bus station and as the bus drove away, it seemed as if Ridgefield was really quite a small place straddling the main highway. A man in a trilby hat got out of a car parked on the other side of the road. He looked at me and we both nodded and walked towards one another. As we neared, he said: "Hi Edward, my name's Frank". He looked and sounded just like James Cagney.

As it turned out, Frank was Mrs Dickson's driver, gardener and general factotum with his wife being cook and cleaner. Yet they seemed more like friends and Frank had charge of her cheque book so that he could pay all the bills. When we arrived at her large timber-built house, I was made to feel most welcome and Mrs Dickson was obviously pleased to see someone from her old home and birthplace, even though our relationship was only by marriage and really very tenuous.

Frank's wife cooked us a nice meal and afterwards he took me for a drive. Although this was a lovely neighbourhood, there wasn't much to see except the huge grounds of a recently-departed multimillionaire who had lived next door.

Mrs Dickson was full of questions about her relations back home, many of whom I didn't know. Sadly, however, conversation was not easy as, apart from failing eyesight, she had broken her hearing aid; still, she was not bad for a woman approaching her nineties.

The next day, Sunday, Frank drove us to "The Inn" at Ridgefield, a most impressive restaurant with a canopied walkway from the roadside to the door. We were met by the owner, a man with a European accent who made such a fuss of us and escorted us to a table, with Mrs Dickson insisting all the time that he must let her pay for our meal! She explained over an excellent lunch that her husband, Stewart, had loaned him the money to get started. It seemed that this part of America was full of people who had enjoyed his help and generosity and their gratitude hadn't died with him.

I caught the bus back to New York later that afternoon and was back in my own bunk that night, having phoned Harry Burroughs and arranged one last evening out before we were due to leave. That last evening was memorable as Harry and Marguerita took me to the theatre where we saw a one-woman show with the popular English comedienne and actress, Joyce Grenfell. The next day our passengers, an American missionary and his family, boarded and we sailed. Two weeks later, we were anchored off Freetown in West Africa, ready to take on our Kroo Boys and start discharging the general cargo we had loaded in the States.

Soon after leaving the United States, we had discovered, much to the captain's annoyance, that we had a stowaway on board. He was a black American who wanted to return to his roots but was to find that it was not so easy.

Ships can be fined for landing aliens and he made the mistake of demanding that it was his right to be put ashore. As he stood well over 6 feet tall, it was almost comical to see our captain, at a bare 5 feet, jumping up and down and telling him that the vermin on board had more rights than he did.

It took several of the crew to drag him down to the baggage locker where he was locked in. It became less comical when the captain had him chained to the mast on deck to prevent him going ashore. He was later transferred to another of the company ships which, no doubt, would transport him all the way back to the United States.

I had already found that it was not uncommon to have the occasional engine breakdown, which would mean us being hove to for a few hours until the ship's engineers managed to fix it. On the voyage across the "pond" this time, however, we had no less than four engine stoppages. During the last, we were surrounded by porpoise. Some of the crew, including the Second Mate, claimed to have seen a 10 ft shark off the bow and this prompted our missionary passenger to get out his Winchester 32 rifle and go hunting.

We never saw the shark again and the ship got under weight but, having got his gun, the passenger leaned over the bow and put another hole in the back of one of the porpoises that were still swimming just in front of our bow.

We doubted that this would kill it but feared that the scent of blood from the wound might result in a shark finishing the job. The crew were disgusted at this wanton shooting of a porpoise, particularly the African seamen and, as if by magic, our friendly travelling companions immediately left us.

By mid-July, we had completed discharging all our cargo from the States, including the Pontiac and Oldsmobile cars in the tween decks. Loading was well under way and our working day had become shorter again, from just 7am until 5pm with Sundays off. We had cooler weather up the Congo and, towards the end of July, were back in Lagos. The 500-passenger company flagship, Aureol, was in Apapa being prepared for her homeward voyage and we were able to join her crew for the luxury of a cinema show.

It was only a short stay in Lagos and we left on the 31st for three days in Freetown where we completed loading, including 200 tons for Bathurst, and lost our Kroo Boys. After a day in Bathurst, we headed for Las Palmas for bunkers, where I picked up a bottle of Drambuie for Father and a bottle of Dry Sack Sherry for Mother before we made a dash for home.

I was now well into motor cars and desperate to get my driving licence. The whole trip had lasted six months and I would arrive home on August 21st in time to enjoy some summer leave and, hopefully, take my driving test.

# CHAPTER 10 - THE QUEEN'S MAIL

I knew that I was due to serve on the company cadet ship Obuasi, but she was not expected home for a couple of months so, after almost four weeks' leave and a failed driving test, I found myself working on the Accra which carried some cargo but, along with her sister ship Apapa and the flagship Aureol, operated the Royal Mail service to West Africa. She carried a full complement of 350 passengers and a round trip from Liverpool took only 30 days and 15 hours. This would bring me back home in nice time to join the cadet ship, which I had been looking forward to.

*RMS Accra*

Compared to all the other ships I had sailed on so far, the Accra was luxury. Whilst we were not allowed to fraternise with the passengers, we were allowed to use the swimming pool between 1-2pm every afternoon whilst they were eating, quite apart from the quick dips we were able to take at 4am after coming off watch. The food was also a revelation even though we, along with most of the officers, had to use our mess room rather than the passenger saloon. The First Mate was a most amiable Irishman and we apprentices were treated more like officers, even though four of us still had to share a cabin.

With most captains not allowing apprentices to purchase alcohol through their bar account, it was common for us to come to an arrangement with the steward at the passenger bar to sell us beer at passenger prices. On the Mail boats, we simply had to go down to the crew bar, affectionately known on all British passenger ships as the Pig, short for Pig and Whistle (pub). Saturday nights were party nights and these were a revelation. It was amazing how many elegantly-dressed and made-up ladies would be seen dancing in a virtually all-male crew. Rather effeminate stewards were not only tolerated, but appreciated, for their good-humoured work ethic but I had not seen this side of their lifestyle before.

We had a limited number of ports of call; Las Palmas for bunkers was livened up by having a team of Spanish dancers performing for the passengers, as well as the services of Frisco and his stalls on deck. After that, there was only Freetown, Takoradi and Apapa wharf at Lagos, where we turned around and visited the same ports again on the way home.

For our time in Apapa, we had the ship to ourselves and could enjoy the film shows as long as the weather permitted, as the screen was set up on the swimming-pool deck.

Whilst in Lagos, we were also fortunate enough to be invited, along with the cadets from the Swedru, to go sailing with Mr Julian Holt, a senior manager of the shipping line who was currently based in Lagos, in a small sailing yacht owned by the company. I had only previously sailed on cutters at Aberdovey and ship's lifeboats, so this was indeed an experience of something that I would come to enjoy again much later in life.

Afterwards, we were entertained to drinks and dinner at his house and games of carpet bowls, before being dropped back at our ships around midnight. I was getting to like life on the Accra and wishing I could do a few more trips on her but it was not to be, as least not yet.

# CHAPTER 11 - A PAINFUL EXPERIENCE

I only had a short leave this time, which was not unexpected after a thirty-day voyage. On the very first day, I discovered that my next driving test had come through; but needless to say, as I had not been good enough last time and had been given no more lessons since, I was still not good enough this time! Being at sea was obviously not conducive to learning to drive a car.

*MV Obuasi*

It was a consolation, however, to at last join the Company's cadet ship Obuasi in Victoria Dock, London. Not being one of the four poor juniors on board, I was berthed in the poop deck accommodation aft, where we enjoyed being in the old crew cabins, half-a-ship's length away from authority. However, we did have to put up with the vibration from the ship's propeller when we finally sailed on November 19. My station was aft as we let go and, with the help of tugs, slipped into the River Thames.

There were no ratings at all in the deck crew, so we apprentices did everything from handling the ropes and wires on leaving or arriving in port to manning the watches, following the same system as any British crew with three watches and three men to each watch, day and night. I was on the 12-4 watch and we did alternate duty so that one man did the first two hours on the wheel, keeping to the course set, the third hour was stand-by which could be spent in the mess room if there was no work to do and the third hour was spent standing on the fo'c'sle keeping a look-out.

There was a telephone, but the traditional signal is one sound of the fo'c'sle head bell for a sighting to starboard and two for a sighting to port, with three rings for dead ahead. The next watch-keeper did the same thing in reverse and the third started and finished his watch on stand-by with two hours lookout between; For some reason, the latter was generally referred to as the farmer! Once clear of land, we trailed the log, a small propeller which turns a clock showing miles steamed.

During the working day, everyone not on the wheel worked with the acting Bo's'un, or senior apprentice, on deck. At this stage of the voyage, after the ship had been washed down, this involved overhauling all the running gear. For a few of us, this involved a race to see who could get the job of going aloft.

It was so invigorating to be aloft in fine weather. Up there, you could spot dolphins and the occasional whale while everyone else was busy on deck. We did have a proper Bo's'un on board but his function was only to keep an eye on us and make sure that the work was always carried out properly and safely. In effect, he had very little to do except report to the Managing Director of the company, who would often come aboard at the end of each voyage and ask how his young 'gentlemen' had performed.

Amongst our passengers on this trip was the British Consul to Senegal, with his wife and two 17-year-old daughters. Despite considerable seduction by our crew, both of the latter appeared to survive the trip to Dakar unscathed. We had a full complement of 12 passengers on the outward voyage and, with nothing else to do, the drink seemed to flow freely. It was no wonder that all fraternization, except for the most senior officers, was forbidden.

We eventually arrived in Lagos and tied up at the quay on December 7 where we saw the last of our passengers. My old ship, the Zini, was alongside and before she left, Second Mate Graham Wilson and I went to Victoria Beach by taxi for a midnight swim. What we hadn't allowed for on a moonless night was that it was pitch black and all you could see was slight fluorescence in the surf to show you where the waterline was. We didn't stay in there for long!

With another colleague, I was shortly assigned the role of night-watchman, which entailed making sure that no undesirables came on board, raising or lowering the gangway as the tide changed and also adjusting the moorings if necessary. We did not, of course, use this time to get some sleep but instead lowered the sailing gig, carried on the afterdeck and sailed down to Tarkwa Bay for a day on the beach and swimming. We still had to stay awake all night but the eggs and bacon left out with the occasional sausage helped in that respect. Having woken the crew, we were then able to get some sleep in the morning, leaving the entire afternoon to go ashore or, even better, lower our sailing gig and sail round to Tarkwa Bay again for a swim. Sadly, we didn't make it a second time - halfway there, I started to get the most violent stomach pain and we turned about for the slow haul back to the ship, against wind and tide. By the time we got back, I was just able to climb the ladder back up the ship's side and get to my cabin before vomiting.

Our Chief Steward, Fred Killick, was in charge of the medical locker and he came to see me. I shall be forever grateful to him. Within an hour, I was on my way to the company office, where I endured what seemed like a pain-filled hour in the back of a car, presumably whilst the necessary paperwork was completed, before driving the rest of the way to the Creek Hospital, where I was swiftly admitted and given a bed. As we were roughly opposite the Creek Hospital in our sailing gig when we started back to the ship, it seemed a pity that we hadn't just come here in the first place.

I had to suffer afternoon visiting before I was examined, but the doctor soon diagnosed acute appendicitis and issued instructions to have me on the table by 9pm that night. I remember being administered some pre-op medication and then the obligatory shave by a Nigerian male nurse, who drew blood as he hacked away with an old Gillette safety razor. I soon forgot the discomfort of that, however, as he washed away the bloody remnants with iodine!

I never did find out if the easing of the pain in my stomach was due to anything they did or whether the offending appendix had burst. Whichever, I was duly on the operating table at 9pm ready for the show to start. Half-an-hour later, the surgeon and his anaesthetist arrived to put me out, both having obviously enjoyed a few whisky-enlivened sundowners to get them ready. I was just glad that they had arrived!

Some of my shipmates came to visit over the next few days and brought clothes and toiletries, together with the usual cheerful, if derogatory, banter that passes for sympathy in England, plus some fruit supplied by Chief Steward Killick. The rest of my gear had been collected by shore staff as the ship was sailing and I could only be thankful that my trauma had happened when it did and not at sea, a few days later. I had one or two more visits by company and port health representatives, not to mention kind ladies who were visiting others in the ward. There seemed to be a camaraderie at work and the other patients kept my spirits up although an extremely strict English matron did her best to discourage all laughter in the ward.

# CHAPTER 12 - A FIRST-CLASS PASSENGER

Just seven days later, my wound was unstapled and I was transferred to the company mail boat Apapa, sister ship to the Accra, on which I was to travel home as a DBS or Displaced British Seaman. Having officer status, I was entitled to a first-class passenger berth and this I insisted on, despite an attempt to put me in a vacant berth in the apprentices cabin, as I knew what that would mean! I was allotted a lower-deck cabin, sharing with a strange fellow who claimed to be a Government entomologist travelling home on leave. He had, apparently, moved out of his official bungalow and lived in his black girlfriend's hut, showing me photographs to prove it. In truth, I hardly saw him as he would spend each night in the third-class accommodation, which in those days was almost entirely occupied by African passengers, playing Ludo and snakes and ladders !!

I was still in some pain and couldn't straighten up when I boarded the Apapa and was told to report to the ship's doctor. His comment when I showed him the scar across my stomach is one that I will never forget. "Which butcher did this?" he said.

However, this did not stop the First Mate searching for me on most days in order to give me a job, either tallying cargo or writing out the crew overtime sheets. But, whether laying by the swimming pool or in one of the lounges, I kept a weather eye open for him and always managed to hide in the toilets until he had passed.

I had to have my meals in the officer's mess but spent most evenings playing Canasta in the passenger lounge with three other young fellows who were travelling home. As I had no money, I tried refusing drinks but they always insisted and I would find the odd pound note stuffed in my shirt pocket enabling me to buy the occasional round. No-one admitted being the mysterious donor, but I did have my suspicions - until his sad death over 50 years later, I exchanged Christmas cards with Bill Oxenbury and occasionally visited him at his home in London.

When we called at Las Palmas for bunkers, I realised that it was great being a passenger. For the one and only time, I was able to go ashore for a few hours although the only thing I remember was the sight of big old American cars. There were so many relics of the 1920s and 30s, still in immaculate condition. Thanks to the dry weather, nothing seemed to rust. It was also a change to have the time to watch the show laid on for the passengers by the troupe of flamenco dancers who came on board.

On arrival in Liverpool, the company mail boats would always discharge their passengers at the riverside berth near the Liver Buildings where there was a customs hall and a railway station, from where they could board trains to take them on to their final destinations. For once, I was able to leave the ship there, to find my parents waiting with the car. Another half -an-hour and I was home, just in time to celebrate the new year. Yet when I visited the pay office a few days later, I found that my pay had been stopped as I had left my ship in Lagos. I had no money to draw, which seemed a little harsh especially as I thought I was on a four-year contract and I had still been away from home. The staff in the pay office told me to claim sickness benefit; when I did, it was a further surprise to find that I was being paid more to be off sick than I was to be at work!

By that time, I had joined our trades union, the Merchant Navy and Airline Officers Association.

# CHAPTER 13 - BACK TO THE REAL WORLD

Given the difference in pay, I would have been more than happy to have a longer sick leave but, just over a week later, I was back on the Apapa's sister ship Accra working by until we sailed on January 17. Being on the 8-12 watch enabled me to take a morning sight each day at sea. This was valuable practice, especially as the Second Mate would lend me his vernier sextant, upon which I would be examined when I was up for my Second Mate's ticket. As we got further south, I was also able to have an occasional swim in the pool, which helped get my stomach back to normal.

This was going to be an eventful trip as we were at Lagos during a visit by Her Majesty Queen Elizabeth II. She was due to officially open the new section of Apapa wharf where we were berthed. We were warned that the Royal party may wish to come on board our ship for afternoon tea, so the ship was given an extra clean and plans were drawn up for the event. The actual visit was on Friday February 10; all the officers had to wear No 10 uniforms and were positioned at different parts of the ship to keep the crew in order. I was stationed at the gangway, which was raised, with the Captain and two of the quartermasters who would lower the gangway if and when we were to have a Royal visit. In the event, the only thing they had to do was lower buckets of fresh water to revive the odd crewman from HMS Sparrow, who had been forming a guard of honour on the quay, when they passed out with the heat.

Our Captain, eyes glued to binoculars, was watching the end of the new sheds for the first sign of the Royal cavalcade. When it appeared, he put the binoculars down out of sight, reached for his uniform cap and instructed the entire crew, who were lining the rails, to stand to attention. It was only when he whispered out of the corner of his mouth "which car is she in?" that I realised how poor his eyesight really was. Of the three cars slowly approaching, the first and last were Jaguar saloons; the Queen and Prince Philip were between them in an open Rolls Royce. I told him this and, as the second blur passed, he gave a smart salute. I suspect, however, that he never actually saw Her Royal Highness or Prince Philip and they never came on board after all!

Another apprentice friend of mine was, I learned later, on another of the company ships further up the quay. His Captain also saluted, knocking my friend's cap off as he did so. I hope the Queen saw it and was amused.

A couple of days later, I was invited to dinner by a gentleman named David Lord, a friend of Bill Oxenbury, who was living in Lagos. We went to a new hotel called the Mainland for drinks and then went to the Ikedja Arms Hotel, where we sat alongside the swimming pool listening to the dance band. There was no apartheid in the British colonies, but Europeans were certainly able to live well despite the heat and flies. At dinner, I was shocked at the way in which some of these educated men sat at dinner and talked disparagingly about their African servants, without regard to the fact that they were standing just behind them. I was to learn later that the wealthy African could be just as bad and was often worse.

The rest of the voyage was uneventful except for my third-year exams, which did not seem too difficult as I was now getting much more time for study. We had some really bad weather from Ushant Island all the rest of the way to the Liverpool bar but arrived home safe and sound and before I knew it, it was the end of February.

Then, I was on my way back to Africa, with a promise from our manager, Mr Millard, that he would try to get me back on the Obuasi for my next trip as she was due to arrive back in the UK towards the middle of April. During the voyage, we heard that she had lost another apprentice who had to pay off with appendicitis, luckily in New York, not Lagos.

I was again on the 8-12 watch, getting lots of practice with a sextant and filling up sight-books. During the first few days out, the weather was still very rough and although I suffered my usual bout of seasickness, which I was by now quite used to, our new purser-apprentice, on his first trip, could not get out of his bunk for three days.

In Lagos, I was able to spend some more time with David Lord, who came on board with two friends to watch the film 'Geordie', which was fairly new and popular at the time. The following Sunday, he took me to Victoria Beach for the day, followed by another dinner at his house, after which we again savoured the delights of the Ikedja Arms Hotel.

On March 26, we were loading passengers, many of whom had motor cars, which we loaded using the ship's gear. They had to be securely lashed down in the 'tween deck cargo spaces, which was to save them being badly damaged, as we would again have severe weather the nearer we got to home. One of the homeward passengers was married to my uncle's sister-in-law, a gentleman who I had known from a child and who lived in Ormskirk. He had been working at a tin mine up-country at a place called Jos when he was taken ill and was being repatriated. As we knew he would be joining the ship before I left home, I was able to take some warm-weather clothing for him. For this reason, I was allowed some time in the passenger accommodation for limited socialising. This was the only time I was able to see Bob Acton until we both arrived back in Liverpool, where I signed off and had a short leave before travelling by train to London, to join the ship I had left so abruptly in Lagos just over four months ago.

# CHAPTER 14 - BEST SHIP IN THE FLEET

At last, I was back on the cadet ship Obuasi, with some of my old shipmates and quite a few new ones, all except two of whom were junior to me. This situation was to change as soon as we reached Lagos when the senior apprentice was transferred to act as uncertificated Third Mate on one of the company's small coastal vessels. By then, I would have celebrated my 20th birthday and be sharing a cabin with the now senior cadet, Charlie Moore, who would become our effective Bo's'un, reporting to the chief mate on the bridge at 6am each day to be told what the day's jobs were to be. As junior, I would have the privilege of an extra hour in bed, before the pre-breakfast chore of cleaning our cabin. As the second senior cadet, I would also become the official lamp-trimmer, which no longer entailed trimming the oil lamps but did mean that I'd be Bo's'un's mate when there was more than one work party, or when Charlie was absent.

We had left our berth in the Victoria Dock on April 20 and instead of wearing officer's uniform and relaying orders, it was dungarees and working gloves as we took in the heavy manilla mooring ropes and wires and made fast the tugs that were to help us move out into the river Thames. Most of us had been on short lifeboat and EDH (Efficient Deck Hand) courses inbetween leaves and working by our ships in Liverpool, which was the normal requirement, together with an appropriate time at sea for becoming an AB, so we had both the experience and qualifications to man the ship and satisfy the Board of Trade regulations.

It was the usual run of ports down the West Coast with the occasional excursion ashore to play football, until we discovered that we had enough enthusiasts aboard to form a rugby union XV at which point the search was on to find a team to play. Much to our surprise, it was at the surf port of Accra that we got the first of our two fixtures.

It took several surf boats to transport us to the beach where the crews had the dubious pleasure of carrying us through the surf and on to dry land. Hopefully, we were preferable to the usual bags of cement which they had to carry. The team we were going to play was, in fact, made up from the management team of the Costain construction company. It was they who were using all the cement that we had been discharging to build the completely new port of Tema which would, sadly, make all the surf boats at Accra redundant within the next year or so.

The fact that they had a rugby pitch was a good indication that their skill level would be so much better than ours, even if we had been fit enough. They beat us easily but we enjoyed the game and the beer which they insisted on making us drink before we had to return to our ship.

Our second fixture was against the European club in Lagos, against whom we had previously played soccer. The pitch was at the Lagos polo ground, which had quite a grand clubhouse. Once again, we were badly beaten but after the game, instead of the offer of six bottles of Star lager to share on the verandah steps before returning to the ship, we were invited into the clubhouse to be supplied with jugs full of beer, sandwiches and an evening of cheerful conversation, bawdy jokes and rugby songs. What a wonderful game is rugby union football.

After we left Lagos, my newly-elevated position meant that I was no longer on watches at sea or had nightwatch duties in port. It was day-work from then on, with Saturday afternoons and Sundays off, except of course if we had to be on stations arriving or leaving ports. It was about then that two elderly sisters were murdered in Ormskirk (the crime is still unsolved as I write) and all the men in the town were fingerprinted. I suppose you could say that I had the perfect alibi, having been over 2,000 miles away at the time.

There was a tremendous sense of pride in our ship, which we were determined to make the best in the fleet. This was displayed whenever we entered port, as the derricks were being raised ready for work to start the moment we arrived on our mooring. On other ships, they would go up in random fashion, one forward and one aft. Obuasi's derricks would rise in pairs, exactly together, starting forward and working aft, both on the foredeck and on the afterdeck.

One of our apprentices, Mike, had been a bugler on the Training Ship Conway and we purchased a second-hand bugle, to which call we would raise our flags at 8am each morning and lower again at exact sunset. Thereafter, the only time that I recall us not doing this was after the First Mate told us not to forget. It was, after all, our idea and not his!

There were other things of which he or the Captain may not have approved, such as our practice of flying a home-made skull-and-crossbones over the poop deck accommodation but nothing was ever said. In fact, when the captain of another of the company's vessels was reported as having said he would not allow it on his ship, we sneaked on board the night before he was due to sail, and fixed a small spare to the top of the main mast. His face must have been a picture when he saw it the next day!

That particular captain's nickname was "Bastard Jack" which was an indication of his popularity in the company. He was also known to have a fondness for growing plants in little boxes outside his cabin. In fairness we had relieved him of his garden one night and while he was aboard Obuasi complaining to our captain about our crew of "brats and hooligans" we sneaked it back. I believe that our captain enjoyed the joke as much as we did. There was a tradition of raiding other ships whilst we were in port and whilst there could have been some truth in Bastard Jack's description of us we never did anything harmful or malicious. It could be that we had missed out on most of the normal teenage years, including young romance and these were our last desperate attempt to enjoy adolescence.

We returned home mid July, berthing first at Avonmouth, close to where the father of one of our shipmates was licencee of a pub called the Ship's Bell. Half of the apprentices were sent home on leave and one of the replacements was duly delegated night watchman, so that the rest of us could hire a coach, in order to sample same of Dad's scrumpy. We were halfway there before someone noticed our night watchman hiding behind the back seats. It was too late to turn back and by the time we got back, all present, if not entirely correct, the ship was still there !

The rest of us had a short leave when we arrived back in Liverpool and I for one was soon looking forward to signing on for the next voyage. We had put a request in to the company for a swimming pool and a record player in our recreation room aft, thinking that at least we would get the latter and indeed, there it was when we rejoined in London. We quickly organised a whip-round, generously added to by Bo's'un George, and a list of our favourite records before dispatching two of our more musically appreciative cadets to the nearest record store. Much to our surprise and just before sailing, we also took delivery of a large bundle of canvas and a sling full of 3" x 3" timbers, together with an envelope containing a set of plans marked "Swimming Pool".

Soon after we left the busy shipping lanes, heading south under sunny skies, we unpacked our canvas swimming pool, no doubt constructed by one of the Liverpool sail-makers. We then enlisted the help of our ship's carpenter to decipher the plans and cut the timbers to size.

It was designed to sit on the main deck, between the ship's side and the cargo hatch and would be held together with removable steel bolts to allow it to be dismantled when we were in port, or carrying deck cargo. It became my daily chore to act as carpenter's mate and we managed to complete building the frame just before arriving at our first port, Dakar in Senegal.

The canvas pool was suspended inside this framework and there was some excitement as we filled it with seawater using the nearest fire hydrant. This took some time as the whole thing was 20 feet long and 12 feet wide. At five feet deep, it held over 30 tons of water and was quite deep enough to dive into and swim. Bo's'n George, who we would rib mercilessly during the voyage, showed us what a good sport he was by joining us aft in our recreation room for a celebratory musical soiree that night, signing several bar chits for 20 beers at a time, along with his own gin and tonic. We collected this beer from the passenger bar in a galvanized bucket and made sure that his drink was at least a double measure. I think he lost count of the chits he was asked to sign and may have had some explaining to do later. Disgracefully, before the evening ended, we carried him up the deck and threw him over the high side of the pool. It was only when we heard a dull thump instead of a splash that we realized that the evening watch had emptied the water out in readiness for arriving at the next port the following morning!

During our stay in Takoradi, where all ships were moored between sets of buoys located behind the protective arms of two breakwaters, my old ship the Swedru tied up at the next berth the day before we were due to sail. After dinner that night, I and another cadet rowed across in our gig to visit old shipmates. We were soon ensconced in the Third Engineer's cabin, exchanging gossip and being plied with cold beers. We were obviously well entertained, because it was almost dawn before we stumbled down the gangway and made our way back to our ship, where we were horrified to learn from our night watchman that we had been raided. The apprentices and junior officers of the Swedru had, to our shame, actually used our own gig and stolen our skull and crossbones flag which, as light dawned, we could see flying from the top of Swedru's mainmast. This did, of course have to be rectified and revenged.

Plans were quickly drawn up and, after a very quick breakfast, two of us again rowed up their port side towards the bow, watched by all of their crew who were not still at breakfast. At the same time, over a dozen of our boys hid in the company launch as, on its way around the harbour with mail, it went from our gangway around the stern to theirs. Within seconds, there were bodies running everywhere and one, who went under the name of 'Watney' Evans, was climbing their mainmast. He quickly untied our prize flag and dropped it down to waiting hands below. The captain chased two men off the bridge and half-a-dozen raced up to the fo'c'sle with Kroo Boys, under orders of the officer on deck, hard at their heels until they jumped off, to be fished out of the water by us in the gig.

Somehow, everyone got back to Obuasi without being caught and our flag was again proudly flying over the poop when we sailed mid-morning, A strongly-worded complaint from the Swedru's captain was sternly passed on to us with a warning to behave more like officers and gentlemen, but I could swear it was accompanied by a twinkle in the eye.

We must have reached a peak of high spirits during this voyage and became more piratical as we worked our way down the West African coast. No company ship was safe and one Friday night, after we reached Lagos and berthed at Customs wharf, seventeen of us crossed the harbour to Apapa wharf and raided five company ships, one after the other.

No flag or noticeboard was safe and even the signs from the ladies and gents toilets of an adjoining passenger ship were stolen. I suppose we were acting more like 12-year-olds than the junior deck officers we were all, hopefully, soon to become. Strangely, the only complaints received were from supervising stevedores on the wharf, where we had created disgraceful mayhem by running up and down, knocking heavy bags of kernels off labourers' heads in the process. This was not something of which we should have been proud. It would have been after that when we visited the "Bastard" Jack's ship, to carry out the more excusable escapade which I described earlier.

My cabin mate and senior cadet, Charlie, had a girlfriend back home whose father worked in Lagos and when he was invited to dinner and to take a friend, I was fortunate to enjoy yet another meal ashore. I have to say, though, that the relationship between master and servants could not have been more different. Our host joked and made his servants laugh and they responded with obvious affection, making our evening a much more enjoyable experience for all concerned.

From Lagos, we went up the Niger delta to Burutu and Sapele, where we finished discharging and commenced loading logs from the huge rafts being floated down the creeks from the logging camps. It was here also that we started washing down and painting the ship.

I remember this visit to Sapele for two reasons; one was the monsoon-type rain which resulted in us having to spend most of our time painting the dry sheltered areas of the passenger deck bulkheads in a fresh coat of white paint, with the other being the mango flies.

When the rain did stop, we hung staging around the bows and stern, clear of all cargo work, in order to apply the topside's black paint and, when it was dry, sign-write the ship's name and port of registry. Sitting on a plank of wood, suspended under the overhang of the ship's hull, we had noticed these huge black flies before but when we were told that the males were harmless but the females were prone to lay their eggs under human skin, we did not feel the urge to discriminate between the sexes, especially as none of us were in the habit of wearing shirts. As soon as we saw one approach or heard the buzz of it, panic would set in. With a full brush of black paint in everyone's hand, you can imagine the scene. At the end of the day, there was probably more paint on us than on the ship.

The rest of the ship's sides and the working decks could not be done until loading was complete but we were determined that our ship would be pristine when we arrived home and everything else that could be done was done as we worked our way back up the West Coast.

Lagos harbour was quite big and sheltered making it perfect for sailing, so we took advantage whenever possible and, with the chief mate's permission, put our gig in the water. The favourite destination was always Tarkwa beach, which was enclosed behind a small breakwater, itself inside the main harbour breakwaters. On a Sunday afternoon off, about half-a-dozen of us sailed the three miles down the harbour and into Tarkwa Bay in about 40 minutes. We had a great day on the beach but hadn't taken account of a strong ebb tide and having to sail into the wind to get back. It took us three-and-a-half hours, using both sail and oars and as it was quite dark by then, the mate had gone off in a port tug to look for us!

There wasn't an opportunity to sail again as we left Lagos and would be busy painting ship on every dry day that we had until we left the last port on our way to Liverpool and home. For all the trouble we caused the Captain and Chief Mate, they never had to ask us to work overtime when there was a job to be done even though we were never paid for extra hours worked.

There was no stop for bunkers as the ship's fuel tanks were to be inspected at the end of the voyage but we did call at Belfast where our deck-cargo of logs was discharged. We were given a coach trip to the Giant's Causeway whilst there, but our evening ashore was memorable for the fact that the town was full of Canadian sailors from a visiting aircraft carrier and two escorts. We couldn't resist returning to our ship and changing into reefers. The uniform cap and Merchant Navy badge, together with the blue raincoat, was enough to reward us with hundreds of smart salutes, considering the poor lighting and general state of the sailors after a night ashore. It was all great fun and when we did arrive in the Mersey on October 24 1956, we were still the smartest ship in the fleet.

# CHAPTER 15 - A PROPER OFFICER AT LAST

My apprenticeship still had over six weeks to run and I still needed another few weeks seatime (on articles) before I could sit my Second Mate's exams, so I had to work by the Obuasi for a week or so until I was relieved. Almost three weeks' leave and a few more driving lessons followed and then I joined the flagship of the fleet, the Royal Mail ship Aureol. As my apprenticeship would be complete halfway through the 30-day voyage, I joined as an Apprentice and an uncertificated Fourth Officer. This enabled me at last to wear a single gold band on my sleeve.

*MS Aureol*

More significantly, with a lengthy period of unemployment ahead whilst at college, this also meant a tremendous leap in pay, up to about £50 per month - the only downside, of course, was that I would start paying income tax.

Unlike the Accra and the Apapa, the Aureol was painted all white above the waterline and, although smaller, with a complement of only 500 passengers, she had the appearance and lines of a proper passenger liner. I was assigned the 12-4 watch and, for the first time, I had an apprentice making my tea when he wasn't manning the weather wing of the bridge.

Unusually for Las Palmas, we were still in blue uniform and it was another day or two, after we left, that the weather allowed us to change to whites. Then it was the usual run to Sierra Leone, the Gold Coast and Nigeria and back the same way. In order to make the best use of time and fuel we invariably arrived at first light, giving my watch an hour or so in bed before having to be up again and on stations; then it was cargo and passenger baggage duties until departure.

As soon as we were on course to the next port of call, it was time for the evening meal which often entailed relieving the watch, either before or after we could enjoy ours. A nightcap and a few hours in bed and hey, it was one bell and time to get up and back on the bridge for another 12-4 watch.

Apapa wharf at Lagos was a welcome break as we would be there for a few days whilst we got rid of the remaining cargo and remainder of the passengers. After a decent night's sleep, there was also time to go for dinner again at David Lord's house and bring him back to the ship for a drink and to watch the film Battle of the River Plate in the ship's cinema. The following day was December 17 and, having completed my indentures, I had to go ashore and officially sign on as a ship's officer.

We had Christmas at sea on the way home and on December 31, landed all our passengers at the old passenger terminal, next to the Princes Landing Stage on the Liverpool waterfront. Later that evening, we were able to enter the Sandon half-tide basin and the clock struck midnight just as the water levels equalized, allowing the gates to open into the dock system proper. We were on stations fore and aft and all ready to let go our moorings. In the 1960's the River Mersey was still a bustling port, with hundreds of ships in the miles of docks, each with a whistle ready to welcome the new year.

There was nothing to do but wait for the noise to abate so that we could hear the orders from the bridge. Gradually, the noise did get less until just one Anchor Line ship in the adjacent dock was left. It was another 10 minutes before the steam ran out, we were able to move and the tugs pulled us through into the Huskisson Dock. The delay was worth it for me when I discovered later that our neighbour, Captain Bill Andrew, was stand-by mate on the ship. Knowing that I was on the Aureol, he had the engineer provide him with a full head of steam and tied the whistle down.

There was petrol rationing at the time and as it was too late to catch a train home, I was offered a lift as far as Maghull, where the family of the Third Mate's girlfriend, who had come to collect him, were having a New Year party. I was assured that others there from Ormskirk would be able to give me a lift the rest of the way home. Unfortunately, they had already left when we arrived and my poor Dad had to get up and come for me at 3am. By then, however, I had already made friends with whom I would spend much time over the next few months while I was at the Liverpool Nautical College studying for my Second Mate's ticket.

## CHAPTER 16 - LIVERPOOL NAUTICAL COLLEGE

You didn't have to pass any exams to be junior officer in a merchant ship, apart from a lifeboat ticket, but most British companies would insist upon anyone from the rank of Third Mate upwards having at least a Second Mate's ticket. In the case of a foreign-going ticket, as distinct from a home trade or coastal ticket, this involved having already had over three years and three months of sea time i.e. time signed on articles (excluding leaves or time working by a ship in a home port), together with a successful week of examinations.

These would include three days of written papers in mathematics, navigation, ship-construction, ship-stability, and English Language, followed by a one-to-one oral examination. This covered safety at sea, knowledge of the publications of reference such as Merchant Shipping Notices and Admiralty Notices to Mariners, a working knowledge of both the sextant and magnetic compass, together with thorough understanding of Regulations for Prevention of Collision at Sea. There were 32 of the latter which included details of the working lights and shapes that all vessels had to carry; for many examiners, these had to be learned by heart. The final part of the examination would involve tests in both semaphore and Morse Code and The International Code of Flag Signals.

For most ex-apprentices, this required at least two months in college to prepare, despite the correspondence course which I had completed over the last three or four years. Early in February 1957, I signed on as unemployed and started my Second Mate's course at Liverpool Nautical College. Life followed a routine of travelling into Liverpool by train every weekday, collecting unemployment benefit on a Friday and having all my evenings and the weekends free, which was a wonderful change. I was able to join my local rugby club and actually began to enjoy the game every Saturday afternoon, despite the winter weather. Perhaps I had been toughened up over the last four years!

During those years, I had never had more than three weeks' leave before being called back to sea, even after seven- and eight-month voyages and I found getting down to study hard going. Girls were a real distraction and my two months at college had stretched to three before I finally applied to take my examinations. I decided to wear a bow tie on the third day of the written papers as it happened to be on May 8, my 21st birthday. Well, I had to do something to mark the event.

The oral examination on the following day was perhaps the most traumatic couple of hours in my life so far, the odd acute appendicitis included. I knew before I was called into the room that my examiner was the most feared of the lot. The figure behind the desk, head bowed over some papers, curtly told me to "sit down." Panic began to set in as there seemed to be no chair provided - I knew things were going to be difficult. Looking around the room, I finally noticed a chair against the back wall and, placing it in front of the desk, sat down.

Eventually, the examiner looked up and asked a question, apparently of a person behind and to the right of me. When I looked and saw no-one there I realized, with growing horror, that he had a cast in his eye and that it was indeed me to whom the question had been directed. He had impatiently repeated it before I mumbled an answer and noticed that, apart from his squint, there appeared to be a hole in his cheek, out of which grew a clump of black hair.

To this day, I remember little of what happened in that room over the next 90 minutes, apart from that clump of black hair and his final, muttered comment that I had passed 'by the skin of my teeth'. I think I thanked him, before escaping to the nearest pub for a steadying drink.

The Signals exam was held fortnightly and I took a short break to recover, and have some extra lessons, before successfully passing that third and final part of my Second Mate's Ticket. By that time, I had learned that I had also been successful with my written papers and had, at last, secured my Certificate of Competency to be a Second Mate. This was duly reported for the week ending May 30 in the Autumn 1957 edition of the Merchant Navy Journal. I had already removed the Apprentice insignia from the collar of my reefer jacket and was now able to sew the single gold stripe with diamond on each sleeve. The next thing was to get another job, preferably on a tramp steamer rather than the passenger and cargo liners where I had served my apprenticeship.

My main reason for going to sea was still to see the world and signing on a tramp ship, which would not be limited to a particular trade route, seemed the obvious way to achieve this. I would also need at least another 18 months of sea-time as a watch-keeping officer before I could return to college and sit my next qualification; to do this in one voyage would kill two birds with one stone. However, finding a British company engaged in this type of trade proved more difficult than I had imagined.

An interview with Ropners at their office in Darlington did seem to go well and a position as Third Mate on a vessel called the Swiftpool, calling at Rotterdam, would be confirmed in a few days. But on my return home, I had a message to call Captain Lloyd Jones at the Merchant Navy and Airline Officers Union. He had been most helpful in securing my end-of-apprenticeship bonus from the Elder Dempster Line, when they had threatened to withdraw it.

This seemed to be because I had, perhaps aggressively, refused to return to their employ once I had qualified. Knowing that I was looking for a berth on a tramp ship, he asked if I had any objections to sailing, not as Third but Second Mate, on a foreign flagship. Without further ado, I attended another interview at an agent's office in Liverpool.

Solely due to my youth, the offer was revised to Third Mate for a short probationary period, but the wages, plus overtime, would still be much higher than on a British ship. I accepted, sending a telegram to Ropners explaining why I was having to decline their offer. This was proved unnecessary when I received a letter the next morning to learn that the Third Officer on the Swiftpool had decided against taking leave and I was free to look elsewhere.

Ropners would obviously have consulted my previous employers regarding my character and I could imagine the telephone conversation between them and Elder Dempster Line, during which they would have been warned of my involvement with a trades union, which the Merchant Navy & Airline Officers Association was; not that it was in any way what you could call militant.

# CHAPTER 17 - SAILING UNDER THE FLAG OF PANAMA

I signed articles on June 24 1957 and joined another old liberty ship named the SS Panamante, registered in Panama. Whilst I already knew that the captain was Yugoslav it was something of a shock, after a tortuous train journey from Liverpool to Immingham, near Grimsby in Yorkshire, to find that I would be the only Englishman on the ship - and that only a few of the crew could speak English. Fortunately, there was a Londoner visiting who had sailed on the ship previously as a radio operator. He had become fluent in Italian, which was the general language used on board. I was encouraged by him and the First Mate, who was from Trieste and had only a smattering of English, to stay and this was a decision that I was not to regret.

The name Panamante was derived from the owner's name, Ante Topic; it was one of four ships he had re-registered when the Yugoslav President Tito nationalised shipping as part of his communist state. The sister ship was named Panamolga after his wife. They lived in Monaco, reputedly as Lichtenstein citizens, but the ships were owned under different company names and they seemed to be operated through offices in both London and New York, where all the cargoes seemed to be arranged.

The ship was discharging a bulk cargo of sulphur. When discharge was complete we were to proceed, in ballast, to New Orleans and the Mississippi River for another 10,000 tons to bring back to the UK where I could easily have paid-off and come home. Instead, I bought a course in Italian entitled How to speak Italian in three months without a master produced by the Hugo Language Institute in London, for the princely sum of six old shillings (30 pence).

Captain Zarko Grgic, like most of the Yugoslavs on the ship, had escaped from Communism under Tito. He must have retained his passport and had managed to gain entry into America with his wife and daughter, with the whole family seeking naturalization. Other Yugoslavs in the crew had been out of the country when Tito gained power after the war and had never returned, so retaining their Yugoslav passports.

Others, mainly those employed in the engine room as firemen/greasers, were sailing on Italian work permits and, without proper nationality, were unable even to go ashore in the United States. Most of the crew were, however, like First Mate Andrea Spetich - from Italy and in particular from Trieste, an area which had at various times been part of Yugoslavia, a fact which accounted for some of the names and variations in spelling.

The Chief Engineer, Jozo Mateljak, had never officially returned to his home in Dubrovnik since being with the British Navy in Malta during the war. Apart from having a liking for bulbs of raw garlic at breakfast, he delighted in singing "My bonny lies over the ocean" in effective but broken English as we enjoyed a beer or two in the evening.

Olivo Ragau, an Italian seaman on my watch, had quite good English thanks to having been a POW in North Africa. He was most amused when I asked him if he had ever tried to escape. "Why?" he said, "Prisoner of war is good, I buy cigarette from American soldier, trade with Arab for souvenir and sell souvenir to American soldier. I make good money. Why escape?"

A rather better English speaker was the relief radio officer, who joined the ship shortly before we sailed. Although not English, he was, like many fellow radio officers in those days, a Southern Irishman trained by the Marconi Company.

Although I had been to Virginia and Maryland with Elder Dempster Lines, this was to be my first trip into the Gulf of Mexico - I was certainly looking forward to seeing New Orleans, even though our stay there was very short. Our first evening was spent exploring places like Bourbon Street which was full of bars and strip joints. Outside each would be a man trying to draw customers in with the cry: "Come on in boys, we got 12 girls (or 24, as we got further up the street) and every drink is a dollar".

The ones we did venture into saw the girls shimmy down the bar, one by one, stripping down to the briefest of briefs before disappearing behind a curtain to return dressed, with the object of persuading one of the clientele into buying them a most expensive drink, which was probably coloured water. This was a temptation which I found easier to forego than one or two of my companions.

The following afternoon, I again went ashore to get a haircut. On the long road down to the waterfront, I passed an open doorway and the sound of music made me look inside, to see a black man tap-dancing to the jukebox. It was a warm day and there would be cold beer at the bar, so I went in to refresh myself and enjoy the show.

No sooner had I ordered a beer than the record ended and the black man picked up his broom and carried on sweeping the floor. It was at this point that I was ordering another beer. I took pity on the only other person in the bar. She had previously asked if I would buy a drink for her and so I offered her a beer. "At least it would be someone to talk to while I finished my drink," I thought. But then, another girl appeared on the other side of me and the barmaid placed another four beers on the bar, including one for herself, insisting that I had ordered them.

At that point I drained my glass, suggested that she called a cop and walked out as she put the beers back under the bar. I have never forgotten the sign over the door which described it as the "Black Cat Club".

I made another mistake that afternoon in finding a barber shop, down on the waterfront, where I had the most expensive haircut and wash ever. My only excuse was that it was a very warm day and the wash seemed like a good idea at the time.

In general, all on board Panamante were much older than me, except for the two junior members of the deck crew and the mess boy, Claudio Mahnic, who was slightly younger. As a Ship's Officer, perhaps a young looking one at that, I decided to grow a beard. It took a while and was not the full set that I hid behind later in my career - it was about a year later, when I returned home, that my barber described it as an "imperial," a comment which did wonders for my ego.

Most of our cargo of sulphur was to be loaded up-river at a place called Port Sulphur. The Mississippi is a delta and and when we journeyed there, it was fascinating to see clusters of small seaplanes along the banks. These were obviously the quickest and perhaps the only means of getting quickly from one place to another. Whilst there, the captain's wife and daughter were to join us for a trip across the Atlantic and back, having travelled from their home in Manhattan.

The Captain's daughter, Rose Marie, was only fourteen but quite a pretty girl and her frequent visits to the bridge whilst I was on watch were obviously of some concern to the Captain. At first, I thought he was worried that I might be distracted from keeping a proper lookout but when I saw the attention and wolf-whistles that she got from the young Italian mess boy, I realised what his true concern was.

The river jetty at which we were moored was quite small and loading was by conveyors, which had limited movement. For this reason, we had to keep winching the ship backwards and forwards as each hold was loaded. This meant that our gangway had to be moved from its normal position on the ship's side to enable access from the jetty, which in turn meant swinging out one of the lifeboat davits to hang off a temporary gangway. Unbelievably, it took our bo's'un two hours to free this davit which, through lack of lifeboat drills, had become completely seized up with rust and paint. It took me another two hours of my own time to free the other davit so at least the port lifeboat could be used if ever the need arose.

There was no uniform, as such, on the ship but most of the officers dressed in the American style and wore khaki shirt and trousers. This included Captain Grgic, although he also wore a peaked khaki hat similar to that worn by an American Army officer; in appearance, he had a distinct similarity to General Eisenhower. He certainly maintained a fairly strict discipline on board which had the crew running when he gave an order. Mind you, it was apparent that most could not afford to lose their jobs. It was also very clear that his main concern was keeping down operating costs and maximising profit for the owner. However, the issue of safety was very low down as a priority and I was never to see a lifeboat drill or fire drill in the ten-and-a-half months I served under him.

The next occasion which showed the result of this was in Hull, where we were discharging our cargo of sulphur using ship's gear and wicker baskets, which were filled by shovel. A stray spark resulting from the steel hook hitting the propeller shaft tunnel ignited the basket which flared up like the head of a match. The sulphur cargo itself did not burn, although any dust was flashed off and the dockers in No 5 hatch swarmed up the ladders to the safety of the deck. Whether it was fear or the obnoxious smell that chased them is not certain but as I happened to be on the spot, I instinctively ran to the nearest hose and reeled it out before attempting to connect to the fire main at the side of the after-mast house. It was then that I realised that the coupling was the wrong size.

Seeing the Italian Bo's'un appearing from the midships accommodation, I called "Nostromo", one of my first words in Italian, and pointed to the problem. "Momento" he called and disappeared foreward, to return a few minutes later with an adapter. While he connected this vital element of our fire-fighting equipment, I directed the hose at the flaming basket.

It only took a few minutes to douse the flames but, by that time, the Chief Engineer had called the men up from the other afterdeck hold and turned on the steam-smothering system, which was designed to smother fire below. Both hatches being wide open, we never even saw the steam.

At the same time, the Second Mate appeared with the breathing mask and air cylinder from the bridge, but was at a loss to know how it worked. The only officer who appeared to do anything constructive, apart from me, was the Chief Mate. With the fire already out, he snatched the hose from my hands just as I saw the Captain appear at the end of the boat deck, looking to see what was going on! Whether this would have changed anything is doubtful but whilst in Hull, the Second Mate, who had stayed for an extra voyage to America, was relieved by a quite elderly Yugoslav who was to stand in until the Captain was sure that my age would not be problem.

Apart from purchasing my language course on Italian, I did manage to make a quick trip home from Hull to see my parents and ease their minds about the ship I was on. The more difficult thing was persuading the ticket clerk at the station that the silver coins I offered were genuine; they had all turned black from exposure to sulphur, even though they had been in my trouser pocket hanging inside the wardrobe in my cabin!

We left Hull on August 25 bound for Brazil, where we were to load a full cargo of iron ore for the States. On the way, we called in at Sao.Vincent in the Cape Verde Islands for bunkers. Filling up with oil fuel only took a few hours, but it was enough time to trade an old pair of trousers and 200 American cigarettes for a guitar, which I had every intention of learning to play before I returned home, as well as learning to speak Italian. Whilst I did, more or less, achieve the latter I left the guitar at the back of my wardrobe, without loosening the strings. This had the unfortunate result, thanks to changes in temperature and humidity as we travelled, of eventually causing it to break in half, putting paid to any future I had as a musician.

This neglect on my part was probably due to the fact that most of my off-watch time was being spent relieving the boredom of young Rose Marie Grgic, either by playing countless games of Canasta or Monopoly. In return, she helped to relieve the boredom of my evening watch for the odd hour or so. It seemed no time before we arrived at Vittoria, which is about five miles up the Rio Santa Maria in Brazil. In fact, we had arrived prematurely, because we had to steam back to find an anchorage and then spent three days awaiting a loading berth.

Rose Marie's older married sister apparently lived in Rio De Janeiro and she, with her husband and two children, had flown to Vittoria for a grand reunion after an eleven-year separation. The Grgic family had a most enjoyable party and even the eldest, a 10-year-old boy, had never met his grandfather before. Although the children only spoke Portuguese, this must have been a very emotional family reunion; certainly, the reason for Captain Grgic's wife and daughter being with us on this voyage became clear.

We had all been looking forward to the first mail from home, as the postman had failed to deliver at Sao Vicente and then found that all mail had gone on to Rio de Janeiro. It had still not arrived three days later, when we finally tied up late on September 15 at a wharf which had a very high wall along its length. Conveyors ran from ports near the bottom of this wall and closer inspection showed that there was a steep hill behind, with the space between them being used as a huge natural silo for the ore that we were to start loading. Originally, Vittoria was not our planned port of call and apart from being a bit inconvenient for the Captain's family, Vittoria was also a disappointment for the rest of the crew, who had all been looking forward to the delights of Rio De Janeiro.

Once alongside, we had a chance to go ashore and found it to be a colourful town nestling between the hills, comprised of a number of small skyscrapers surrounded by shantytown. Most of the people seemed to be of mixed blood, with Portuguese, Africans and native Indians the main ingredients. The results were a lot of extremely pretty girls but the same could not be said for the men. Apart from a number of bars and a single cinema, the place was pretty dead and we were not sorry to leave two days later, bound for the port of Philadelphia. However, these orders were also changed and we finally received our mail at Baltimore. Before that, we were to go through a hurricane as we entered the Caribbean.

The waves were huge and it didn't pay to think too much about the bulk cargo of nine-and-a-half thousand tons of iron ore in the holds. The motion of the ship was so bad that I ended up lacing myself into my bunk to make sure I wasn't thrown out as I slept; drawers had to be tied shut and everything moveable was lashed down. When I was on watch, we heard an SOS on the radio from a large German sail training ship called the Pamir, which was overcome by the heavy seas and sank about two hundred miles to the north of us. We were too far away and too slow to be of any assistance but, fortunately, I heard that most of the crew were saved.

We finally said 'farewell' to the Captain's wife and daughter after our cargo was discharged in an incredibly short 24 hours and we then spent a further day waiting for more bad weather to clear before a 7am departure on Monday October 6. I was not the only one with bleary eyes; on the previous evening, my fellow shipmates had given me a guided tour of the strip bars that I had been too young and certainly too poor to frequent on my previous visits to Baltimore. The female strippers were just as lewd as those in New Orleans and the male audience just as appreciative. Only the Mississippi drawl was replaced with a Maryland drawl. The evening had finished in the usual way, with a huge cheeseburger or hotdog, apple pie and coffee.

According to the BBC news programmes that I was able to receive on my shortwave radio during our trip back down to Norfolk in Virginia, where we were to load coal for Rotterdam, the pound sterling was in danger of being devalued; consolation lay in the fact that my salary was in US dollars so I was, in effect, due for a pay rise.

Two days later, we were laden with coal and on our way back across the Atlantic. We passed through the English Channel, round the Hook of Holland and up the river to Rotterdam where we discharged our cargo. Less than two days later, on October 25 we were in ballast, out to sea and on our way back to the Mexican Gulf. Our Irish Radio Operator had paid off and we had a Yugoslav in his place but by this time, I was more than comfortable with my foreign shipmates.

Our next port was Pensacola in Florida where we were to load most of our cargo of scrap metal. This was done using electro-magnets on cranes, which dropped the large, heavy chunks of iron into a metal channel which was carefully positioned to shoot them into the corners of the hold. There was little for the ship's officers to do other than watch bumps appearing in the ship's hull as it was dented from the inside, although some time was spent gazing offshore at an old Navy aircraft carrier watching a procession of small seaplanes practice landing and taking off from its decks.

The longshoremen all seemed to have mahogany-coloured wrinkled faces and a Lucky Strike or Camel cigarette in the corner of their mouths, looking for all the world like the waterfront crooks and murderers out of Hollywood films. Their language, when you could understand it given the deep southern drawl, was unrepeatable and largely racist.

It only took about 15 minutes to walk into the town, which was clean and pleasant with the usual dimly-lit bars in which only the bottles were illuminated. All the drinks were ice-cold and if you asked for something without ice, the barman thought you were mad, German or English. I seemed to be in good company. Things were not so good for those members of the crew who were sailing without proper passports, however. Having been refused a visa, they were swiftly picked up by the immigration authorities and returned to the ship after brief and illegal trips ashore. The speed of this process may have been due to the US Navy base responsible for training the offshore fliers already mentioned.

We completed loading and were at Panama by early-December, en route for Honolulu where we were to take bunkers before continuing across the Pacific Ocean to discharge in Japan. Panama seemed the obvious place to post all my Christmas cards, as it was a major port of call for the fast passenger liners travelling between the Antipodes and the UK. Being bound for Japan put paid to my early promotion as the rather elderly Yugoslav Second Mate would not be signed off and sent home until we arrived back in a European port nearer home. Although we were alongside awaiting our turn for canal transit, no shore leave was given due to rioting by the local people.

It appeared that the Panama Canal was the only place in the world where the Master of any ship wishing to transit the canal had to hand over complete control of the vessel to the pilot; normally, the safety of a ship and its crew are always the responsibility of the Master and a pilot is only employed for his local knowledge and advice. In this case, however, it was not difficult to imagine that, should the huge twin locks which allow large vessels to climb up to the central lakes of Panama be breached by a collision, it could result in catastrophic flooding of the lower coastal regions.

In our case, the pilot was an American, which was not unusual as the Canal Zone was under the control of the United States and its very existence was a result of their need for a quicker passage from one side of North America to the other - or at least, one which could be open all the year round.

Apart from their expertise in ship-handling and procedure, these pilots also had to be able to issue helm and engine orders in every language so that no mistakes could be made in translation on ships like Panamante, where the Yugoslav captain would have to translate from English to Italian for the helmsman. The system was not perfect, of course; the Pilot once made the mistake of issuing engine orders in Italian to yours truly, when I was manning the engine room telegraph. Fortunately I had, by that time, become used to the Italian terms for whatever order he was giving.

These giant locks were truly impressive with small diesel engines, running on tracks along the high-side walls. When the lock gates finally closed behind us and they started flooding, the ship rose fast up the steep walls on either side until we could see another ship going down, just as quickly, on the other side of one of them. All the time the small mules, as they were called, were tightening the wires keeping us in position until we were ready to move into the next lock and go up again. The biggest of these sets of locks were like three giant steps and we were to be lifted up again like this before we finally entered the lakes at the top of the Panama Canal Zone. The process was reversed on the other side of the isthmus, as we went down using more locks before we reached sea level and emerged into the Pacific Ocean.

When out of sight of land, the sextant was the only way of charting our position and the First Mate would attempt to use the stars, both at dusk and at daybreak when there was still a horizon. Each morning, the Captain and other navigating officers, including me, would take an altitude of the Sun to get a longitude and run it up to noon, when the Sun was at its zenith, to cross that with a latitude. The Captain then compared all our positions and usually decided that his had to be the right one, although they were all within a mile or so of each other.

For some time, we had all had our reservations about the Second Mate, who seemed so unsure of himself with the sextant but always produced a position similar to the rest of us. One day at noon, the First Mate decided to test this. He put a blank in the telescope of the bridge sextant which the Second Mate was to use at noon. When he agreed with everyone else's reading, it was obvious that either his eyesight was poor or working out a sight was beyond him.

From then on, he was relieved of navigating duties and whenever we were in busy sea lanes, the First Mate and I doubled up on watches. This was exhausting but did earn me a lot more overtime. Sadly, we were en route to the other side of the world and too far from home to pay him off. Air travel was not then as easy and cheap as it became later and it would take us almost five weeks, travelling at a bare 10 knots, to reach Honolulu. I was the only person on board who actually went ashore as the crew's visas for the United States, at least those of the crew who had qualified for them, had run out.

My exception was made on the Master's orders, in order to visit the shipping office on ship's business. I never knew whether this exception was with the permission of the immigration authorities, but it enabled me to buy an Hawaiian shirt as a souvenir before we sailed. Even if my visa had still been valid, our eight-hour stay in port would not have been long enough to visit Pearl Harbour. That was a shame as I was never to visit the Hawaiian Islands again and we were back at sea that evening.

The following morning was Christmas Day and I was surprised to find a bottle of whisky on the table when I came down into the saloon for breakfast. Christmas dinner, if I remember, consisted of the usual pasta followed by a steak, with our cook's rather special gateau to finish off. Apart from that, it was just like any other day.

We had another two weeks at sea before we arrived in Japanese waters having travelled all the way across the Pacific Ocean, mostly out of sight of land and barely seeing another ship. I had been used on British ships to using the sight of another ship to practice signalling using the Aldis lamp. Usually, the messages flashed between two ships would reveal the name of the vessel and where she was bound before signing off with a 'goodnight' or 'bon voyage'. They also helped to relieve the boredom of the long night watches. The procedure for calling another vessel was to send series of 'AA's in morse code and the response after each received word would be a single long flash or a 'T'. One dark night, I continually tried to attract the attention of an approaching vessel on a reciprocal course to our own until we finally passed one another about a half-mile apart. In some frustration at the ignorance and bad manners of my opposite watch-keeper, I sent a rather rude two-word message as he was disappearing astern. The letter 'T' that I received in reply brought a smile to my face, which made all the effort worthwhile.

Another odd experience on this ship followed messages picked up by our radio operator

*SS Panamante*

74

*The Author sporting a Third Mate's braid leaning on a rail*

*Home of Liberty Bell at Philadelphia*

*Famous Red Squirrels who share the home of Liberty Bell*

*Approaching Manhattan skyline*

*The streets of Manhattan and Central Park*

*Cleopatra's Needle, Central Park*

*Boating on Central Park Lake, New York*

from his counterpart on another ship in which he claimed that the Captain of his ship had gone mad and was trying to kill him. Another message seemed even more desperate, saying that he was barricaded in the radio room with the Captain trying to batter the door down. His ship must have been fairly close to our position as, the following day when I was on watch, First Mate Andrea Spetic came racing up on the bridge as an American warship coming up rapidly astern was calling us on the Aldis lamp. When I answered, it was to ask the usual questions as to our name and where we were bound before overtaking us and disappearing over the horizon. Soon, we picked up another message confirming that it was the radio operator who had gone mad and that he was being transferred to a passenger ship for transporting to hospital. It was often said at sea that the time alone in the radio room, spent listening to Morse Code all day, was a recipe for mental problems - this seemed to be the proof.

Daytime watches during these long sea voyages, outside busy shipping lanes, were also kept from being quite so boring by the Officer of the watch being encouraged to carry out maintenance work, with the Captain paying occasional visits to the bridge as an extra pair of eyes. We had no automatic steering, so a helmsman was always present and work was usually confined to paintwork around the bridge and boat deck, allowing for a frequent quick scan of the horizon.

On one occasion, I even applied white lead and tallow to the mainmast stays using a boatswain's chair, with Spetic lowering me down on the winch. At least I could still make my quick horizon searches from that elevated position. This practice would have been frowned upon on British ships, but it did worry me when I saw the Second Mate painting the afterdeck scuppers during his afternoon watch when the Captain may have been enjoying his afternoon siesta.

We finally berthed early one morning at buoys in Osaka harbour, using the services of a Japanese pilot. The international nature of the English language was again demonstrated as helm and engine orders were issued by him in English, to be translated by a Jugoslav into Italian for the man at the wheel. As usual, I was operating the engine room telegraph and further translation was unnecessary.

Almost immediately, barges started to come alongside, filled with men who were to start hauling scrap, by hand, into the square of the hatch, ready to be picked up by steel grabs which they had fitted to our own lifting gear. Barges would be filled and towed away to be replaced by more barges. We never saw where they went but we knew that the steel would be quickly melted down into plates and beams to feed the growing shipbuilding yards, one of which was building a new ship for our owner just across Osaka Bay. Each morning before daylight, the barges would arrive and, apart from a 20-minute stop at lunchtime, the work continued relentlessly until late evening.

The Japanese workers were very polite and their foreman made a point of bringing me an English newspaper each morning which was most welcome, if almost a week old. In return, I would give him a beer or some cigarettes. I complimented him on the way his men worked so hard and his response was that Japan was a poor country and they had to work hard, which made me think of the rather different attitude displayed by dockworkers in Liverpool.

He seemed then to find it necessary to say he liked the British, describing us as gentlemen. I found it hard to believe him but the Japanese do seem to have a sense of honour despite their war record with Allied prisoners. They did, however, complete unloading 10,000 tons of scrap iron in about two weeks.

Time ashore was limited due to the long hours spent working cargo but also because of the need to attract the attention of a harbour launch as we were some distance from the wharf side. This was made worse by some very inclement weather, with high winds persuading the Captain to order all night stand by deck and engine room staff, in case we broke our moorings.

I did, however, manage one part-afternoon ashore, during which I bought myself a cheap, yet high-quality, camera and a similar pair of binoculars, together with presents for my parents which would be sent by post. Altogether, while we were in Japan I managed just two evenings ashore. My companions were Italian, who seemed to be highly-regarded, having been allies of a sort to the Japanese during the war. I had an enjoyable time in the nightclubs of Osaka but it did amuse me that when we had a meal, my shipmates all ordered spaghetti!

Inspection of the holds after discharging our cargo revealed the damage sustained as a result of the shooting of heavy and sharp chunks of metal, at speed, into the corners during loading in America. Watertight bulkheads were no longer watertight, with welds broken and holes through the steel, all of which had to be welded up before we could sail, in ballast, for our next port of loading.

This would be another long sea voyage. It took almost a month to reach the city of Vancouver in British Columbia, where we were to load a full cargo of sawn timber. It came as a surprise to see dockers arriving, smartly dressed at the ship, in a taxi and carrying a bag containing work clothes. After work, they had facilities for washing and changing clothes again and leaving just as smartly-dressed as they had arrived. We were berthed alongside, so it was easy to go ashore and sample the local beer but it was another surprise to find that unaccompanied men were not allowed in the lounge bars. Instead, we had to use what could only be described as tiled drinking halls which resembles public toilets rather than bars. There were, in fact, no bars as such, only tables and chairs. As soon as you found somewhere to sit, two glasses of beer were placed in front of you, with an empty glass being replaced almost immediately by a full one. This was not my idea of a convivial drink.

Soon after we arrived, I was given another special assignment by the Captain. One of the crew was experiencing some trouble with his plumbing after our sojourn in Japan and I had to take him to the General Hospital in Vancouver for a blood test. I found it fascinating to watch the nurse having great difficulty in finding a vein prepared to give her the blood sample she required; at least, until I started feeling very strange.

The next thing I remembered was laying on the floor surrounded by faces and having a spatula poked in my mouth to make sure my tongue was still in the right place. I still blame the hospital's central heating, coupled with the roll-neck jumper and heavy coat I was wearing. It was February, after all, at a similar latitude to home and with bitterly cold weather outside.

Despite everything, Vancouver was a most beautiful city in a most beautiful setting, with Vancouver Island across the Sound in front of us and snow-topped mountains behind. We only part-loaded in Vancouver itself before entering the Fraser River to reach a place called New Westminster, where all the dockers seem to either have a cabin in the woods for hunting, a boat for salmon fishing or both. One night, I was invited to the home of a customs officer named Woolf for dinner. His wife was English and the invitation probably only came because I was also English.

His house was quite large and, like most of the others in the area, was built entirely of wood except for the fireplace and chimney. The house was on stilts with a garage underneath which housed the central heating boiler. The house also had a flat alongside, which was rented to a newly-arrived immigrant couple from East Ham in London, who already loved it here. I was told about a British ex-merchant navy man they knew who had joined the Canadian Mounted Police and was now captain of a small coastal ferry. He was taking men and their horses up the Sound to patrol in the far north, then bringing others back to take their leave in Vancouver. For a while, I decided that perhaps I would emigrate to British Columbia instead of New Zealand, which I had still to visit!

Our final loading port was Victoria on Vancouver Island, which was even smaller than New Westminster. It had just one main street and a store, in front of which was a large totem pole. Our cargo of sawn timber was bound for the west coast of the United States along with that of another company ship, the Bimini, which had followed us from Japan. I had an opportunity to visit when she arrived and met my opposite number, a Yugoslav, who was happy to transfer with me. This seemed a possible solution to the question of National Service, for which I now seemed to be eligible as I was on a foreign flagged ship and therefore no longer exempt. The Bimini had a British Master and radio operator, who confirmed that they were on British Articles and that the ship was registered at Nassau in the Bahamas which then was a British territory, flying the good old Red Ensign. There was to be more about this later.

Just prior to leaving our final port, I was on the quayside, having noted down the ship's draft to enter in the log book as usual, when the Captain shouted down to me "Never mind, I fix". It was only when we developed a quite severe list to port two days before we were due to arrive at our bunkering stop in California for fuel that I realized what he meant. On our way down the western seaboard of the United States, we passed San Francisco at night and just managed to make out the lights of the famous bridge before we were passed.

Of course, we were overloaded and as our stock of fuel oil, stored in the double bottom tanks, was used up so our centre of gravity had moved up and we were becoming top-heavy. By the time we arrived at our berth near Long Beach on March 8, the list was so severe that locals were asking me, when I went ashore, if we had been in a collision. Needless to say, the vessel righted herself as the oil refilled our tanks and the Captain had earned his extra bonus. Long Beach was just next door to Los Angeles and, of course, Hollywood. The temperature here, at 94 degrees Fahrenheit, was a lot different from Vancouver.

A letter from home suggested that a friend of my father's, who I had met several times, was in America with the current contender for a World Championship boxing title, Hogan Kid Bassey. My father's friend was sponsoring the boxer and the letter said the pair would be in Los Angeles that very day, prior to the fight. I had also met Bassey once before and watched him train at a gym in St Helens. My father's friend had passed on an invitation to contact them if I was ever in the area. With only about 24 hours before sailing, this seemed impossible until my brainwave.

I telephoned the Los Angeles Times newspaper office from the nearest callbox and ask for the sports editor to see if he could tell me which hotel the Bassey party was using. He was happy to tell me that they would be in Santa Barbara at the Hotel Miramar but sadly, he advised me that they had stayed in New York for an extra two days in order to do a television interview and would now arrive tomorrow afternoon, So my efforts were to come to naught and a meeting proved impossible after all.

We sailed for Balboa and the Panama Canal the following morning, with the consolation that we were at least on the way back into the more familiar waters of the Atlantic. The canal transit was just as impressive north-bound and we were soon heading across the Caribbean en route to our first port of discharge in the USA, Baltimore. I had told Captain Grgic of my need for a transfer to the Bimini and he promised to try to facilitate this through the New York-based company superintendent.

Arriving at Baltimore, we were given our temporary visa which would last a month. It was not long before we sailed for our next port of Philadelphia, arriving at the end of March. Hopes of being able to watch the Hogan Kid Bassey fight on television never materialized. If I did learn who won, I have long since forgotten and early April saw us en route for Newark in New York State. Having warned them of my coming by letter from Panama, it was so nice to see Harry and Marguerita Burroughs again and we had a couple of evenings together. On one of those, they took me to the theatre in New York where the wonderful Joyce Grenfell had a one-woman show; her humour proved just as popular there as at home.

We were almost fully discharged when Captain Grgic suggested that the New York office were not inclined to let me transfer. I asked him, as it was critical for me, if he would mind me approaching the Superintendent directly to explain my predicament. He could hardly say 'no' and when I did arrive at the office, I found that there was no objection at all to my request. My transfer was confirmed the very next day and it was obvious that my leaving Panamante was not to the Captain's liking. I was often called upon to help with his letters to the owner which were always in English, as were all the log book entries, so I cannot say that this was all due to my abilities as a navigating officer.

As it was, I had to complete all the paperwork myself, which included signing off, collecting all the pay I had accrued whilst on the Panamante and preparing my watchkeeping certificate, which Captain Grgic thankfully signed, as I would need that document before being allowed to sit my next exam. This was because the voyage was not included in my British Seaman's discharge book, which also acted as a British Seaman's passport. Before leaving, I had decided to open a bank account in New York.

As the only American bank I had really heard of was the Chase Manhattan, I set off to look for it. It was a most imposing building and when I entered, the junior official who came to interview me at one of the desks in the huge marbled hall suggested, rather imperiously, that they couldn't open an account for less than $1,000 - he was obviously surprised when I produced that sum in cash. In the end, I picked the money up again when he didn't seem to know the procedure for withdrawal in the United Kingdom.

I walked out and found another bank down the street called The Seaman's Bank for Savings. This seemed much more appropriate and they were certainly more helpful. This was to be my "car money" when I got home and further devaluation of the pound could only be to my advantage.

I had realised that my entry visa would also expire before my next ship was due to leave, so I sent my luggage right through on the train but arranged to make a short stop in Philadelphia, home of the US Immigration offices. Having explained my situation and produced the necessary papers, I was surprised to have my request refused, proving that even America had its share of jobsworths. However, another official, hearing my accent, interrupted his colleague. He had been in England during the war and after recalling the good times he had spent there, asked if I knew any of his old acquaintances. Blighty may be a lot smaller than the United States but his understanding of England suggested that it didn't extend much further than his old base. Nevertheless, his friendly help meant that my application was accepted and I caught the next train to Baltimore, with a new visa safely in my pocket.

# CHAPTER 18 - BACK UNDER THE RED ENSIGN

I joined my new ship, SS Bimini, yet another "Sam Boat," shortly before my 22nd birthday. I celebrated with Gibson the radio operator, the same man who I had met when he was visiting the Panamante in Immingham and who helped persuade me to stay. We were loading a bulk cargo of coal for the Continent, where he was to be relieved as he was looking for a shore job where he could use his languages, which now included Yugoslav. The Master, Captain Ewing, was a decent and likeable Scotsman; he was obviously pleased to have another British officer on board, which would still only make the number up to three. He expressed some surprise that I was still Third Mate, until I explained the circumstances as they transpired on the Panamante. We were to get on well and hopes for my long-awaited promotion were rising when we arrived back in European waters.

We arrived at our first port of discharge, Rouen. This was about a third of the way to Paris, up the River Seine, after a brief stop at LeHavre, where both the First and Second Mate paid off and my promotion came at last. This meant that, among my other duties, I was now in charge aft for berthing and letting go our moorings, with the new Third Mate taking my place on the bridge. I would also become navigating officer and have to look after the giro compass. Added to that, I would have the 12-4 watch at sea. This was not the best for sleep, as nights were split in two and there could be no afternoon siesta. However,

*The Author sporting a beard and the gold braid of Navigation Officer*

the downside was made up for by having the satisfaction of sole responsibility for the ship when everyone else was asleep, except of course for the Able Seamen on my watch. Our new radio operator was a young Scot who joined in Rouen, so I replaced one English friend with another Scottish one, while the new Yugoslav First Officer would also become a friend. Of the Engineer Officers, I had also become friends with the Second Engineer who, although in his fifties, was young-hearted and had a very English sense of humour.

I was to learn that the River Seine, like our own River Severn, had a tidal wave or bore, which travelled a long way up-river twice a day. We were on a river berth and, as luck would have it, we were there during a full moon when the bore would be at its fiercest. This would require us to have the engines on standby, with a pilot on the bridge and manning our moorings.

A sharp watch was kept down river and, as the tidal wave appeared round a bend, the pilot ordered full astern on the engines. This sometimes resulted in our stern spring wire parting but it took some of the force as over 16,000 tonnes of ship and cargo were given a lurch forward. Sometimes, the forward spring wire parted but at least it kept the ship on its berth as the shock wave passed. Parted wires would be replaced and we were ready for the next time. This limited our time ashore but, apart from a few bars, there was little to see ashore without taking a long bus ride.

Our giro compass had been switched off on arrival at Rouen and I was ordered to restart it the day before departure. Never having done this before, and never having had to learn the peculiarities of the giro compass, I found the operating manual and, following the instructions, switched on the power. I waited for critical revolutions to build up before releasing the clamps which had been holding everything in place. To my horror, the whole giro began to tilt and, despite all my strength, I could not stop it. I could see that an arm carrying the wiring would be smashed so, in desperation, I switched the power off. This stopped the gyroscopic forces (something I would learn about later) and I was finally able to pull everything back into position and replace the clamps, again using all my strength. It took a giro engineer, who arrived in a small Citroen van, to discover that the rev counter was faulty. It was a pity that no-one had warned me but, from then on, I let the revolutions build up to well over the recommended amount before I attempted to take off any clamps.

Our new Third Officer introduced himself as Jean Francois de Bosset. He was the owner of an apartment in Toulon, a villa in Algiers and a British Second Mate's ticket from Southampton Nautical College. He had joined the ship with a bicycle, which had a small petrol engine in the back wheel, together with 1,000 duty-free Gauloise cigarettes. Most of what he claimed seemed unbelievable and said for effect and this was borne out when he first entered the saloon for dinner. It was normal in the company ships to do the continental thing and say 'priatno', (Yugoslav for 'good appetite'), both on entering and leaving, with all present responding in similar fashion. When Jean entered, for each meal, we would be regaled with "priatno, buono appetito, bon appetit, good appetite, gentlemen", all repeated again on his departure.

After our cargo had been discharged, we left the Seine on June 4 bound for the United States, to load another bulk cargo of coal. We arrived in Newport News, Virginia 15 days later. There was an Elder Dempster ship alongside which I would have loved to board in search of any old shipmates but, sadly, the ship was just leaving as I got there. I did manage a quick word with someone with whom I had never sailed, but knew as a friend of my

Father's back home in Ormskirk and who was leaning over the rail as they slipped their moorings.

A bulk cargo of coal does not take long to load in Newport News, but I was able to spend a few evenings ashore in the company of our Second Engineer, with whom I had developed a good friendship. He was a most interesting man, born in France with an Italian mother and Yugoslav father, who had spent the war years in a German prison camp and who had a White Russian girlfriend in New York. As a result, he appeared fluent in Yugoslav, Italian, French, German and Russian, together with Spanish and a smattering of Portuguese. It seemed as if he could go into any bar on the East Coast of the United States, see a European girl behind the bar and quickly pick up her accent before ordering drinks in her own language. The result was excellent and friendly service, coupled with the odd free round of drinks. Happy days.

Just before we sailed for Civitavecchia in Italy, my last ship Panamante arrived at the anchorage, probably to take our berth as she was to follow in our tracks with another load of coal. We didn't have a Purser or a Chief Steward, so I had carried out the job of preparing crew lists for immigration, crew overtime worked and ship stores requisition lists for the ship chandlers and the like on Panamante. This was work for which I wasn't paid as it was described as being to the benefit of the crew rather than the owner. Now I was also working out the crew wages and I knew that, with overtime, I was at last earning £100 per month, a tidy sum in 1957. My bank account in New York was growing and buying a decent car when I got home was now a distinct possibility.

I had also just learned that the requirement rules for sea-time had changed at home, allowing for a minimum of 12 months between Second Mate's and First Mate's tickets but maintaining the same total of 36 months between Second Mate's and masters. As it was, I already had 12 months under my belt and I realized that I could now pay off whenever I wanted.

Having passed Cape Vincente many times going to and from West Africa, I was looking forward to passing from West to East and going through the Straits of Gibraltar and on into the Mediterranean. There would also be a chance, as we were going to Italy, to practice my Italian with more than just the ship's crew, who would invariably reply in English, which they were perhaps even more keen to learn.

We arrived at Civitavecchia at the beginning of July and there was no delay in getting a berth. It was morning and the unloading of cargo started right away so I decided to practice my newly-acquired language skills by asking one of the foremen stevedores what hours they worked and how many days it should take to complete discharge. He told me that they worked a normal eight-hour day and that it would take about ten days, which meant that we should have plenty of time to visit Rome which was only about an hour away by train. Best of all, he asked me if I was from Trieste, which suggested that my Italian was fluent if with a Triestino accent.

The day after we arrived in Italy, Captain Ewing called me to his cabin and gave me a set of delicate Japanese carvings including a rickshaw, a horse-drawn cart and a junk-like sailboat complete with crew, made from what appeared to be bone or ivory. He then handed the ship over to his relief, another quite elderly Scot named Captain Wilson (who turned out to be in his early-seventies, unused to serving on foreign-flag vessels and not a pleasant man) before leaving the ship to go on leave.

Some of my shipmates, although Italian, had never been to Rome, so when we had a day off, I went with three others to the ancient city and we hired a taxi to have a quick tour of the sights. In Rome, there was plenty to see; all I really remember, apart from lots of ancient buildings and statues, were the catacombs, the Coliseum, the Trevi Fountain, The Spanish Steps and of course, The Vatican. When we arrived at St Peter's Square it was full of children and Pope Pius XII was greeting them on the balcony, so it was opportune (or just lucky) that we were there for that occasion.

The following day, I was charged with taking crew passports to the American Embassy in preparation for a return to Virginia for yet another full cargo of coal, so I had another chance to do a little shopping and enjoy sitting in a pavement café and enjoying some pasta and wine, just off the Via Nazionale, where I bought some classical Italian sandals. These sandals were worn, on and off, for the next 50 years before being discarded but the warm memories of that first visit to Rome have remained with me!

When we left Italy, bound for Newport News and another load of coal, our new Captain ordered a lifeboat drill. In the event, this was probably just as well, as we discovered that the gravity davits, which were unlike the usual radial davits on Liberty ships, were faulty; instead of both rolling down to suspend the lifeboat over the ship's side ready for embarkation, one of the davits shot back inboard, leaving the boat laying diagonally across the boat deck. It took us half a day to get both davits back in the raised position; we never had another lifeboat drill and, even more fortunately, never needed to use the lifeboats!

Another duty of mine was running the bonded store, the contents of which were purchased by the Captain and then sold to the crew when the ship was outside territorial waters. This bonded locker was filled with beer, spirits and cigarettes which, under Captain Ewing, had been sold at just above the purchase price, merely to cover breakages. The officers had been allowed one bottle of spirits a week and the crew just one case of beer, or wine if we had any; there was no limit on cigarettes. This all changed under Captain Wilson, who allowed the crew unrestricted purchase but doubled the price of everything, thus making a handsome profit for himself.

He expected me to help him alter the way things were done on the ship, in line with what he had been used to on British-registered ships. When I suggested that this would be too difficult and probably self-defeating, he ended up accusing me of, amongst other things, conspiring with the Yugoslav First Mate against him. Although he asked me to stay for at least another voyage, I had already determined that I would pay off when we returned to Europe. The situation between us would obviously get worse and, as I already had enough sea-time to sit for my First Mate exams, I advised him that I would insist on paying off in Europe well before we arrived back in Newport News to take on our next cargo of coal.

Our short stay in America was uneventful and I was glad when we were fully loaded and able to get back to sea. Once again, we were heading for Italy where it was to be one of five ports, Savonna, Genoa, Spezia, Livorno or Civitavecchia for discharge. Despite having thrown a coin in the Trevi Fountain, it turned out to be Genoa where we arrived on August 30.

One final drama was to unfold as we arrived at our berth when the First Mate left the foc's'le and returned to his cabin to find money and other financial papers missing. We had never experienced any theft on the ship and suspicion fell on the last crew member to join, Jean Francois DuBosset. When it was reported that he had been seen running ashore soon after leaving his post on the bridge, he was questioned but failed to persuade the Master that he had not taken anything and stashed it ashore. He was paid off and left the ship that day. My relief was due to join the ship the following day but the ship was still short of an deck officer when I left.

The company always required that European crew waited till they arrived in Europe before paying off, for obvious reasons of cost. I had signed on Panamante for a minimum of 12 months in accordance with Panamanian Articles, after which travel expenses were paid by the company.

Captain Wilson, perhaps still resentful of my "lack of co-operation" used the fact that I had only joined the Bimini 4 months earlier as an excuse to refuse to pay my fare home. He even suggested that I should find alternative accommodation before catching the train to Paris the following morning. Needless to say, I took no notice, but did have an evening ashore with the radio operator, who had also decided to pay off, on August 30 1958.

We started the evening at a seaman's mission which turned out to be a favourite place for local girls to practice their English. Having paired up with two signorinas and sampled the local beer, we decided that we needed to go no further. My new friend for the evening was a most attractive blonde girl with what then would be considered a quite daring dress, but who drank nothing but milk. Just behind the table where we were sitting was a large table full of British seamen who, it was easy to tell, were from Liverpool and apparently from a MacAndrews Line ship.

I had been practicing my Italian on my new friend, but it must have been when my companion started to balance glasses of beer and milk on her bosom that I began to hear comments from behind us. Leaning back in my chair, I put on the best Scouse accent I could manage and said "aryerdoinarlritelads?" Their faces were a picture as one of them mumbled: "you certainly are". Any hopes I had for an extended evening were dashed at 11pm when my new friend's father arrived to take her home and the radio operator and I made our way back to the ship!

I turned in that night, excited at the prospect of travelling home the next day. But sleep would not come so, in desperation, I picked a book out of the bookshelf in my cabin to help calm myself. The book I chose was called Moon in Scorpio and the British Seafarers Library Service label in the back showed that it had probably been there since the vessel was purchased by Mr Topic. The remarkable coincidence was the map of my hometown and surrounding district revealed inside the front cover. An historical novel, the book featured the whole of West Lancashire. I finished it on the way home, when my mother read it before half the ladies in the town came to borrow it.

The following morning, I had to buy my own ticket for a couchette berth for myself and Sparks (as all radio operators were then called) at Genoa ticket office. On boarding the train, we found ourselves in a compartment with a female English teacher who had been working the summer holiday in Italy, an Italian lady going home to San Remo and two young French girls bound for Dijon. I had sent my cabin trunk separately to be collected at Victoria Station in London, but our other belongings were in the luggage car.

We got talking to the English teacher, but the trip was otherwise uneventful until shortly before we reached San Remo, when the Italian lady put her magazine down and reached under the seat for a string bag. Then, without expression, she took off her blouse, carefully folded it and placed it in the bag, from which she had taken some material which proved to be a sack dress. This was duly put on over her head and, with some wriggling, down to her knees. Her skirt was duly unfastened and appeared from beneath the sack dress when she carefully folded and placed it, with the blouse, in the string bag. It wasn't until she had picked up the magazine again and found her page that she look up to find us all watching; That was the moment when we all laughed with her and any ice in the compartment had been well and truly broken. Sadly, we lost our happy Italian lady at San Remo where her seat was taken by a rather older French woman who, like us, was bound for Paris.

When the train halted at Lyon, we all had to squeeze into the corridor while the attendants lifted up the seatbacks on each side and pulled another bunk down above that , thus giving us a six-berth compartment instead of six seats. I had taken the precaution of bringing a small bottle of rum and those of us who were old enough had a small bedtime toddy before laying down with the pillow and blanket provided.

We would all have enjoyed a good night's sleep if it hadn't been for the stop at Dijon, when the two young French girls awoke in a panic, jumped out of bed, threw their suitcases out of the window, picked up the skirts that had been removed under the blanket and flew down the corridor and off the train. It must have been another ten minutes before the whistle blew and the train pulled out of the station. It was only when we got off at the Gare de Lyon that the French lady discovered that her bag had also been thrown out of the window at Dijon!

The English teacher, Sparks and I had tickets which meant catching another train from the Gare de Nord, so we decided to share a taxi and get the driver to take in a few sights of Paris on the way, as we had plenty of time. However, it wasn't quite the same as a leisurely stroll down the Champs Elysee and it all went too fast for us to remember anything.

There was nothing else eventful in the train journey to Calais or the ferry to Dover where we went through Customs. I had taken the trouble to type out a list of things such as 'camera' and 'binoculars' and my requisite allowance of alcohol and tobacco, which seemed to be appreciated as I sailed through without having to pay anything. My look of satisfaction was picked up by the Customs officer at Victoria station, where I collected my cabin trunk; it resulted in me having to open it for a thorough search which, of course, found nothing.

I took a taxi to Euston Station and deposited my bags in the Left Luggage before travelling straight to the address in London where the Olga Steamship Company was based in order to collect the balance of my pay and claim the travel expenses, refused by Captain Wilson. This was paid without question and, without prompting, the Superintendent suggested that they knew all about Captain Wilson. He wished me luck with my exams and was kind enough to offer me a job if I ever wished to sail with the Company again.

After transferring my things from the Left Luggage office at Euston Station to the guards van, I boarded the train just carrying a briefcase containing my papers plus over £250, a small fortune in 1958. To top it all, I did what sailors often dream of and sat next to a pretty girl. With the rashness of youth, however, I stupidly left my briefcase on the luggage rack while I took her to the bar for a drink. Fortunately, it was still there on our return!

I had been away from home for a fourteen-month voyage, sailing on two different ships, through the Panama Canal and across the Pacific Ocean, so I had plenty to talk about but I never did tell my mother that I had taken a pretty nurse called Jan for a meal in Liverpool before travelling the last 13 miles back home, where I arrived late on the evening of September 1 1958.

# CHAPTER 19 - BACK TO COLLEGE

During my few weeks of official leave before starting college once more, I arranged to withdraw my savings from New York. They amounted to $1,400, still only equivalent to £500, as there had been no further devaluation after all. I bought a one-year-old Ford Anglia (Registration number NWM 29) and became a man about town. Going to parties and seeing my new girlfriend meant that I would take longer than some to pass my First Mate's ticket but I felt that I had earned some fun.

My friend Mike Coghlan was also at college for his Second Mate's ticket and we often met after tea on a Sunday to go for a drink in a popular pub in Maghull. After one such evening, we were in good spirits and looking for somewhere else to go so Mike suggested a house not far away. He knocked on the door and asked if we could come in. "What have you got?" was the reply. We said: "Half a case of beer and some Babychams", the latter then being a popular drink with the girls. The man who welcomed us turned out to be Des Laidler, later to be my Best Man when I got married (although I had not yet met the girl destined to oblige).

From then, it was a regular routine of college and taking Jan out during the week, playing for a junior team at Ormskirk Rugby Club on the Saturday afternoon as soon as the winter season started, then going to a party (often at Des Laidler's), getting up late on Sunday and meeting Mike for a drink on the Sunday night, before starting again at college on the Monday. It was no wonder that I took almost twice as long as I should have done to complete my studies and, of course, I had to see out the rugby season before going back to sea! Only later did I realise how badly I treated the lovely Jan by ending our relationship as abruptly as it started.

My success was listed in the Merchant Navy Journal for the week ending April 2 1959. I ended a seven-month sojourn at home with all my money spent and a small debt to pay back to my ever-forgiving mother after I had managed to secure a ship bound for Australia and New Zealand, where I was still looking to end my own particular odyssey.

## CHAPTER 20 - BACK TO FOURTH MATE

Gaining a Certificate of Competency as First Mate gave me a knowledge of the gyro compass, which would have been useful when I served as Second Mate on the Bimini but it would be another couple of years before I could use it on joining my next company. I had rather optimistically tried Orient Line, P & O Line, the New Zealand Shipping Company and Port Line in my quest to cross the Pacific, before I was finally accepted with immediate effect by the Shaw, Savill and Albion Line.

*The MV Delphic*

New Zealand sounded like an ideal place to settle in order to get away from cold, wet Blighty. By far my longest periods at home had been whilst studying for my tickets, each time during the winter period, with the only consolation being that I was able to enjoy more than the two games of rugby in succession that were possible in the normal period of leave. My qualification and experience so far seemed to deny me a job with the first two companies mentioned above and there were no immediate vacancies in the next two, so I was grateful for the opportunity to start earning again after enjoying my time at college perhaps too much!

A few days later I joined the MS Delphic in Victoria Dock, London for a couple of weeks working by, as the Australia-bound cargo was being loaded. We were signed on Articles on April 13 for the short voyage back to Liverpool and again on May 5, before I spent my 23rd birthday en route to Port Said and the Suez Canal. Even though I had sailed as Second Mate previously and now had the added qualification of a Mate's Ticket, it was apparently the company's practice for newly-joined officers to serve in a more junior capacity for at least one voyage, so I found myself back as Fourth Mate. I still had my own watch and it meant that the First Mate had no watch-keeping duties, so could devote his time and energy to controlling ship maintenance and the loading and discharge of cargo.

As with Elder Dempsters, we were loading general cargo but the holds were mostly capable of being refrigerated for when we are homeward-bound, carrying frozen beef, lamb and butter. Only the shelter deck was solely used for ordinary, un-frozen cargoes. Unlike

Elder Dempsters, the bulk of the ships in Shaw Savill did not carry passengers.

Eight days later, we were one of a convoy of ships at Port Said waiting to start our transit of the Suez Canal. Apart from taking on board special searchlights, which were carefully hung over the bow to shine on each bank during the night hours, we also received a Canal pilot. Ever since the Suez Crisis, when the British lost control of the Canal Zone, the re-opened Canal used a variety of nationalities for this purpose and I discovered, when joining him for an early lunch in the saloon, that our pilot was Yugoslav. He answered my greeting of "Priatno"(good appetite) before uttering a surprised " how you know that?". I explained and we were friends from then until he left the ship. I discovered later that the ship's log books had all been examined by Egyptian officials and that if our ship had ever visited an Israeli port, we would have been denied access to the Canal!

Whilst at anchor, we also had visits from con-men, sleight-of-hand artists and a variety of traders selling goods of often dubious nature, not to mention a barber who boarded with the tools of his trade and a box for the customer to sit on. He introduced himself as "Scouse", in the broadest of Liverpool accents and, as an inducement to those without money at this stage of the voyage, offered a haircut now with payment on the return voyage. It was only on another occasion, with a crew signed on in London, that I realized he was capable of using whichever accent was appropriate.

As the southbound convoy, we entered the Canal as soon as the northbound convoy cleared, using our searchlights until first light. As we proceeded, the local people walking along the banks were gradually left behind. Eventually, ship by ship turned into what was called the cutting, where we stopped and moored to bollards port side to until the main Canal was clear. After a short wait, we were presented with the strange sight of masts, then funnels and finally, as they got closer, the hulls of the next northbound convoy moving through the sand of the desert. When they were finally passed, passenger ships, cargo ships and oil tankers, we were able to let go our moorings and continue southwards towards the Bitter Lakes. Here, we passed yet another northbound convoy, anchored in order to allow our continued passage through the rest of the Canal to Suez where our searchlight boxes were cut loose, to be retrieved by launches. We finally said goodbye to our pilot, who would doubtless join another ship for the voyage back to Port Said.

From Suez, it was a short run down the Gulf of Suez until we entered the Red Sea, suffering temperatures of a blistering 96 degrees Centigrade in the shade on our way to Aden in the Yemen, where we arrived three days later for bunkers. This was also a freeport and a place where we would be surrounded by "bumboats", full of mainly Japanese-made cameras and binoculars. Our stay was only brief and, within hours, we were continuing on our way to Trincomalee, in what was then Ceylon, to load just enough tea to allow us one evening ashore. Here, we enjoyed a few cold and expensive beers in a colonial building that was more of a European residence than a hotel.

Mr Williamson, our radio operator, was from Aughton, near Ormskirk. At 60 years of age but seeming older, he suffered badly from arthritis in his hands. This was not bad enough to stop him using a Morse key, but writing was often difficult and I was able to write a few letters home for him. I also discovered that I knew his son from my time in the Boy Scouts.

Just under a month after leaving home we were in Fremantle, near Perth, for a few days. From there, we travelled across the Great Australian Bight to Adelaide. Both places were very pleasant but seemed small, not like Melbourne where we arrived on June 14, although our berth was actually in the neighbouring port town of Geelong. The State of Victoria had strict licensing laws, meaning that all the bars closed at 6pm leaving not only us, but also the locals, with only the cinema to visit. Early on, I discovered that this was to our benefit.

Soon after the shore-to-ship telephone was connected, it rang. When I answered it, a female voice asked if we were having a party on board. The following night, we had organised some taxis to pick up the girls from the local nurses' home and were able to create our own evening of innocent revelry in the engineers' smoke room, leaving the other, smaller, officers' smoke room for less noisy conversation.

Although the crew were always sober when at sea, I discovered that our captain's rule on this subject did not apply when in port. A distinguished war record had resulted in him being decorated and the evidence of this, kept in his private papers, was shown to whoever he found to drink with.

One evening, when I was on cargo duty, our elderly radio operator was sent to summon me to the Master's cabin. This was to offer me a drink which, despite a respectful refusal as I was on duty, was insisted upon. I agreed to take a small beer.

Although we were used to the sound of the captain firing a catapult at the ship's funnel while at sea, I had never actually seen the weapon until he produced it and offered me a bag of his usual ammunition (nuts) with the invitation to have a shot!

When I asked for a target, he offered the calendar which was hanging on the small corner wall of his cabin. I rather cheekily asked him which date to fire at and promptly missed the calendar and the wall. He then produced a revolver from the safe in his night cabin for me to hold while he looked for ammo (fortunately without success) so I quickly finished my beer, thanked him for his hospitality and returned to the deck, leaving our poor radio operator with him.

Later in the voyage, having a final drink after being ashore with a fellow officer, he appeared in my doorway, inviting us both up to his cabin. Manners led me to invite him to join us and after finishing of a good third of a bottle of whisky, he left; but not before saying that the trim beard I sported suggested an untrustworthy nature and ordering me to shave it off. When I suggested that the God himself had a beard, his parting shot was "Jesus Christ, now you are taking the Lord's name in vain"! Drink aside, he was still an effective Ship Master and was always sober at sea.

As it was mid-summer at home, so it was mid-winter in Australia and though not what we would call cold, it was certainly woolly-jumper weather. In some ways, I was reminded of America and its more open society, together with the multitude of commercial radio stations operating alongside the state system which we relied on at home. Either way, it was good news that the British Lions rugby union side had just beaten Australia again, in the second test at Sydney! The more common national game in Western Australia was Australian Rules Football. I had been able to attend a game in Perth, but was not impressed. The game takes place on an oval pitch, with 18 players a side wearing strips which show off their biceps despite most of the action consisting of the ball being booted from one end of the pitch to the other, before hopefully ending up between two of the four posts on each goal-line. I never did figure out the system of scoring.

We must have spent about a week discharging general cargo at Melbourne before leaving for a four-day stop in Sydney in New South Wales. I say "in" Sydney because our berth was almost under the fabulous Sydney Bridge and within easy walking distance of the city centre. The bars were open until 10pm, which meant fewer on-board parties but made it a great place to visit, if still not warm enough to swim at Bondi Beach.

While in Sydney, I met up with an old friend from Maghull. Graham (Mike) Coghlan had also just joined Shaw Savill Line and was serving on the Arabic. We were able to have a night ashore together and, after the pubs closed, called in a coffee bar called the Caribbean. The young man who served us seemed to have a speech impediment and I soon realised that he was, like my brother, deaf. Although unable to hear, he used lip-reading to understand people and he had learned to talk, which explained the apparent impediment. When I explained my connection with his world, he said his name was Victor and that his father owned this and four other coffee bars. We were then introduced to almost everybody in the place, including his sister and the staff. We were made a fuss of until they closed at 1am.

Mike's ship was sailing the following day but I was invited to come back the following evening. This time, after closing the coffee bar at 1am they took me to a night club called Chequers where alcoholic drink was available late. We enjoyed the floor show and partied until 5am; although I had to drag myself from my bunk at 8am, it still seemed worth it and we sailed later that day.

The huge, sheltered harbour itself was most impressive, both to enter and leave. We passed small bays and beaches all the way and the two days it took to travel north up the coast to Brisbane in Queensland saw another decent rise in temperature. Although upriver, our berth was again close to the city centre which was becoming a welcome feature of the ports in Australia. Alas, we didn't have much time to enjoy the delights that Brisbane had to offer before again travelling, for two more days, north to Townsville, less than 20 degrees of latitude south from the Equator and seriously warm.

The buildings in Townsville had a real colonial look to them and the bat-wing doors seen in so many American cowboy films showed the way into bars where the beer was icy-cold and served in glasses that were wet with condensation as you drank from them.

The holds had been cleaned and prepared for the frozen cargoes and we had now started loading for home. After five days I was glad to leave as we sailed south, back down the coast to a place called Gladstone. Although a small place, there were special berths there for ships loading coal for export, which gave a different and slightly grimy impression that was more reminiscent of Europe. Fortunately, this was not a cargo we would be loading and our stay there was only short. It was only recently that I learned how the discovery of coal in Australia had allowed the boom in trade, with better access for coal-burning steamships travelling from Europe.

By mid-July, we were back in Brisbane for a more enjoyable four days where we could get to know the place and its people a bit better. The ship's officers were in charge of cargo stowage and the frozen beef, lamb, offal and butter that comprised the greater bulk was much easier to plan and load than general cargo. The main problem was stowing it in such a way that it could be discharged in the right order for the ports for which it was destined while ensuring that the ship would remain stable. Too much top-weight and too little oil fuel left in the double bottom tanks on the way home could be a disaster.

Sadly, we were only back in Sydney for the day, so I only had time to pop into the Caribbean coffee bar and missed the promised 'homeward bound' party. A couple of days later, we were back in Melbourne to finish loading. Cargo plans were completed four days later and put ashore just before we set off on the eighteen-day passage back to Aden for bunkers and then the Red Sea. We had some of the really bad weather for which the Australian Bight is well known, which resulted in some damage, before we finally passed Fremantle and crossed the Equator via a gentle Indian Ocean, finally arriving in Aden on August 23.

It wasn't until we arrived at Suez and entered the Canal that the days became a little cooler and we became part of a north-bound convoy. By September 3, we had started discharge of cargo in Malta where there was an opportunity for a brief trip ashore. The historic and picturesque city of Valletta seemed to be full of forts and churches, all built in local stone so that it was difficult to see where the cliffs ended and the buildings began. Caves at water level formed bombproof berths for small warships, the place was full of naval personnel and I was sorry to have to leave as we prepared to cast off for the last leg of our voyage back home to the port of Liverpool. Once back in the UK, we signed off articles on September 15 1959, only for me to sign on again a few days later as Third Mate for the short trip up to Glasgow.

Whilst in Glasgow, the Second Mate and I went ashore for the evening and found a small but pleasant bar called the Ritz Lounge, where the barman, who sounded Italian, was entertaining the customers with conjuring tricks between serving drinks. As I had not spoken to him before and it was my round, I caught his attention and asked him for two more beers in what I had been told in Italy was a good Trieste accent. He answered in Italian, served the beers, told me how much they cost and we exchanged the usual pleasantries in Italian before he enquired "Hey, you're a Scouser, eh". It turned out that he had been "Maitre de" at the Palace Hotel in Birkdale and somehow detected the slight Liverpool accent that I had picked up years before whilst working for Elder Dempster Lines. We both saw the joke!

We were only in Glasgow for three days before sailing back to London, where I was able to pay off and travel home on the train for a short period of leave.

I was able to get in a few games of rugby, suffered as a result and enjoyed driving my little Ford Anglia, before travelling back to London three weeks later to join my next ship. This was an older vessel named Karamea which had almost completed loading in the Royal Albert Docks. I signed on October 23 and sailed next day on a voyage to New Zealand, via Curacao in the South Caribbean Sea for bunkers and then another 300 miles to the Panama Canal.

*MV Karamea*

Before reaching the warmer weather of the West Indies, however, we endured some heavy seas. To my amazement, the usual bout of nausea decided to leave me alone - after five years at sea, it looked as if I was getting my sea legs! By November 5, I was certainly well enough to drink a toast to my brother Basil on his birthday. We left Cristobal on November 11 and headed into the Pacific Ocean, with another six-and-a-half thousand miles to go before we reached Auckland. This was my longest sea passage so far and we had only a glimpse of Pitcairn Island on the horizon as we passed south.

We berthed at Auckland on December 4 to find that the wharf was just at the end of the main street. With all the pubs closing at 6pm, however, we were again in demand for parties. This time, our guests were an enterprising group of girls, some of who worked in the various shipping offices in the port and who had access to crew lists. It was a bit over the top when the equivalent of one of our Sunday tabloids printed a piece about Auckland being "Sin City" due to the shipboard parties, but they did at least say that there was no prostitution in New Zealand - it was easy to see why.

The publicans apparently approved of the 6pm closing time as they sold as much beer in the last hour, including "carry-outs" as they would sell if they stayed open all evening. The only downside seemed to be the empty bottles and bottle-tops to be seen on the bottom of ponds in the local parks. The other notable aspect of life was the popularity of radio serials, including 'The Archers' and one serial entitled 'The Woman Who Dared to Love' which I recalled also hearing in both Australia and South Africa. Despite the attraction of the radio programmes, hiring a car for the day showed me what a really beautiful place New Zealand was.

Whilst in Auckland, I bumped into a couple of people I knew from Elder Dempster Lines. They were both working for the Union Steamship Company which traded between Australia and New Zealand, were well paid and were obviously making a life for themselves in the Antipodes.

Most of our cargo was for the North Island, including the port of Wellington and the small Mount Maunganui, with the rest for Dunedin, Lyttleton and Timaru. Even the small ports, however, had a small hotel or bar. In keeping with the standard set by the Captain on my previous ship, the Master of the Karamea had a particular habit when in port. Never a particularly pleasant shipmate when at sea, he could play the piano and, when ashore, he would start a singsong in whichever bar he was in before, at closing time, inviting the whole bar back to his ship for a drink.

The first we knew of this was a demand for any spare drink we had in order to supplement his stock; then, we would hear the sound of a tape recorder coming from his cabin. The tape consisted of him telling jokes and the subsequent sound of him laughing at them. His guests, however, were only allowed one or two drinks while they listened to his tape, before being told he was going to bed; those who were reluctant to leave were swiftly told to b***** off. That was when we all closed our doors and pretended to be asleep until all went quiet and normal activities resumed.

All the holds had to be cleaned and readied for loading our frozen cargo, which was mainly lamb and butter. That started with us back in Auckland, followed by Port Charmers and Timaru in the South Island, where we could see the people on the beach as we worked. Life seemed so relaxed and laid-back; apart from going to the beach, they fished and followed the races, with many of the horses owned by syndicates of dockers. Loading was completed at Gisborne, Napier and then Wellington, all in the North Island.

We had to supervise and mark the stowage with ports of discharge; God help anyone who entered the hold with dirty shoes which might mark the white linen wrapped around each carcass - they were quickly told off by a Kiwi docker with the comment that he had relatives at home who would be eating it.

An 18-year-old member of our crew got himself in trouble in Wellington, not only for getting back to the ship at 5am one morning, but for not being in a fit state to start work on deck an hour later. It was a bit unreasonable, however, to report him to the police and even more unreasonable of the Captain to insist that if he didn't report to the duty officer by 10pm each night, the police would be called.

It was still summer weather in New Zealand as we left on February 10, still in the white uniform which we had been wearing for months. On a more or less reciprocal route to that used outward bound, it took us three weeks to travel back to Cristobal and the Panama Canal. A few days later, on March 5, we were bunkering again at Curacao and back in the Atlantic on our way home, docking at the same berth in the Victoria Docks which we had left five months earlier. I paid off on March 20 and travelled home by train, anxious to change my car for a brand new one.

# CHAPTER 22 - A NEWER SHIP AND A NEW CAR

I traded in my old car, NWM 29, just before I was ordered to Glasgow to join the MV Canopic for a few days working by before I signed on home trade articles on April 19. This was for the short coastal run back down to Liverpool where we finished loading, finally signing foreign-going articles on May 3, before leaving for another trip to Australia. My new car, a new-design Ford Anglia, wasn't ready before we sailed so my father agreed to collect it and I was to be back in debt again, if only for a short while.

*MV Canopic*

Apart from it being my 24th birthday a few days after we sailed, the passage to and through the Suez Canal was pretty uneventful. The Mediterranean gave us pleasant sunbathing weather but the Red Sea gave us temperatures of 101 degrees Fahrenheit in the shade and a scorching 120 degrees in the sun. As we were travelling at 17.5 knots, at least it didn't take us long to reach Aden for bunkers, where I purchased a remarkably cheap "17-jewel movement" watch for just £5. Another three days would see us back in the cooler southern hemisphere and heading for Fremantle.

Adelaide followed and then Melbourne, where I took my new watch to a jeweller with the object of selling it for a profit. The jeweller, an elderly Jew with his eye-magnifier already in place, took one look and said 'Aden?' I said 'yes.' He said "£5?". I said 'yes' again, thanked him and walked out.

Sydney and Brisbane followed, where we finished discharging our outward-bound cargo. My old friend Derek Davies, from my scouting days, would have just got married to his lovely Edith by the time we reached Adelaide so I sent a congratulatory telegram from the ship on the afternoon of May 4, which would arrive by 10am that morning. It was just like being on a time machine!

We left Brisbane at the end of June and travelled up the Great Barrier Reef to start loading 38 tons of copper ingots and 9 cwt drums of uranium in Townsville, which was less than 20 degrees from the Equator and very hot, even in winter. At least there was a cinema there and I recall seeing a British film, "These Dangerous Years," starring Frankie Vaughan. I remember it mainly because it was filmed in and featured my home port of Liverpool.

We were to visit a couple of ports I had not been to before, including Bowen, just a little way back south as well as a place called Wyndham. Bowen was pleasant, like a smaller version of Townsville but not what you could call memorable. Wyndham was something else and would come later, after we had returned to and then left Brisbane and Sydney, where I finally managed to climb the "pylon lookout", which was as far up the Sydney Bridge as you could go at that time. We also visited Melbourne, with a brief stop at Fremantle. We were now almost fully loaded and faced a long coastal voyage rounding the huge area of Western Australia to the very border with the Northern Territories in an area known as the Kimberleys.

Wyndham lay at the head of an inlet, about 60 miles from the open sea in an area known for saltwater crocodiles. There was a wharf which could take two ships, complete with a narrow-gauge railway line which formed a loop connecting it to a meatworks. This contained the frozen quarters of beef and boxes of offal which we were to load. This meant that the crew had to check the number of pieces loaded into each sling, in its rail truck, before it was transported to the ship, lifted by our derricks and tipped into the hold where it was neatly stowed.

The ship's writers, apprentices and deck officers all had to take turns and spend time in the loading bays at the meatworks and I got to know the foreman in charge quite well. Well enough, in fact, to join him in the evenings to indulge in the gambling that went on under cargo lights on tables covered in green baize cloth. The game was always "twoeys", often played in Australia using two pennies but played here using two dice, each showing three heads and three tails. Bets were taken on both dice resulting in a pair and an awful lot of shouting went on. As a change, three dice could be used for the early-death version. The foreman and I played as a team and usually came away showing a small profit. The foreman also expressed interest in my new watch and we eventually agreed a price of £15. He then told me he would have given £25 and I told him I would have taken £10, so we were both happy.

There was little else for the seasonal workers there. They lived in barrack rooms on site and there was only one pub and a post office/shop, with a few houses for the permanent staff. It was too hot in the summer and the place closed down. There was another pub called the "six-miler" because it was six miles away. At weekends, some of the men would catch small crocodiles (by hand, so as not to spoil the skins) which they would kill and then stuff, to sell or keep as souvenirs.

The foreman had also given me a full tour of the meatworks and I was in demand from others in the crew, acting as their tour guide. The cattle were kept in pens over the road at the rear and, one by one, they were chased up a ramp to the top floor by the stockmen where, once in a small raised box, they were carefully pole-axed by a large Australian using the biggest maul I had ever seen.

Only one blow was needed and he would open a side-door for them to slide down onto the main working floor. In groups of six, they would then be processed, ending up in quarters, each in a clean muslin bag, before being wheeled into the freezer-rooms like a rack of coats on a rail. It took about 14 days before they were fully frozen and ready for shipment. The barefooted men doing the processing would kick the offal down through a hole in the concrete floor to be packed and frozen, but I never asked to see that operation.

Seeing the stockmen, in their wide-brimmed hats and cowboy dress, did however awaken a desire to see them at work. After asking the advice of my friend the foreman, I went to see the head stockman to see if it was possible for me to go out with him when he had to restock the cattle pens, which was done every three or four days. He was an obliging sort and it was arranged that I could go out during the following afternoon on my day off.

When I arrived, he had a grey pony ready for me, all saddled up. He had even found an old pair of "strides" as my white uniform shorts were obviously highly unsuitable for riding. I didn't tell him that I had never been on a horse in my life, but felt confident that all the John Wayne films I had seen were sufficient to see me through. He and another stockman went on ahead, leaving me to follow with a colleague of theirs called Steve. Fortunately, Steve was always in ahead and didn't see my awkward attempts to encourage forward movement from my unfortunate steed. Instead, he would half-turn in the saddle and say "give 'er a good kick in the guts, mate. She's a lazy bar'stard, that one".

No amount of kicking encouraged faster progress over quite stony ground and then we came to some clear flat ground, where it was a different story. The horse, clearly determined to teach me a lesson, took off like a rocket and I spent what seemed like five minutes laying on her back before hauling myself upright using the pommel. Having at last picked up speed, I was not going to pull on the reins; at least, not until I saw the high fence looming up ahead!

Now, I couldn't make the horse slow down and when we reached the fence, it turned to run alongside it, trying to rub me off. It didn't work and I was able to lower my right leg again and find the stirrup. After that, we seemed to be friends and I enjoyed a few more gallops.

Eventually, after travelling about a mile, we rounded the red-layered mountain that lay at the back of Wyndham and came to a huge herd of cattle taking water from large troughs, which were fed from a corrugated-iron water-tank. The head stockman was already counting heads with his opposite number in charge of the herd, whose men, mainly Aboriginal, were cutting out those cattle which we would be taking back to the meatworks. The sun was hot even though it was winter and, being on horseback, I was able to put my hand in the water which seemed almost hot enough to brew tea.

With the count agreed, we started back round the mountain. I was delegated to ride with Steve and another older Australian, who told me that he had done this job all over the world, including in North America. He told me that I would be able to say that I had herded cattle in the Kimberleys when I got back home!

Riding right behind the herd, I was struck by the smell of the cattle and also the sight of all the black ticks which seemed to cover their bony-looking rears. From this angle, they didn't look to have enough meat on them for a Sunday roast dinner. This was not surprising, though, as they had probably been driven over 200 miles to get here. Eventually, after a lot of whooping and shouting, we arrived at some high fences which funnelled our charges into the pens ready for what was ahead of them. About 600 head would keep the works going for two or three days.

Apparently, the centre of Australia has thousands of square miles of grazing country that belongs to no-one but the distance from suitable ports makes it impractical for raising cattle. Having a light aircraft and a two-way radio was essential just to survive.

Remarkably, an afternoon in the saddle had only resulted in a mildly sore bottom and two days later, with another afternoon off, I was playing the cowboy again, this time with a little more confidence and more respect from my steed. The same could not be said from my friend Steve. On the final drive into the pens, I noticed a small stray racing back the way we had come. Without a second thought, I wheeled my horse round and gave chase.

More thanks to the horse than to me, we turned the animal and drove it straight back into the herd. Instead of praise, I got the exasperated response: "We just cut that one out, it was too small". My rueful look was probably the butt of some humour in the pub that night!

Word of my exploits must have got round the ship because at least two other members of the crew were to follow. They included a young AB off my watch who, I was told later, had caused the head stockman some concern as he was seen hanging on some poor animal's mane and tail, trying to stay on. Safety was his responsibility and he would never have let him go had he known that the lad had never ridden a horse before. I kept quiet and bought him another beer!

We were in the pub until closing time and as we stood outside, he suggested going somewhere else. As it was a Saturday night, this seemed reasonable, but we didn't know where to go. "Steve's place" was the answer. Apparently, it was halfway to the "six-miler" so he flagged down a taxi. Before we got in, he asked the driver if he had any tucker, at which point the vehicle's boot was opened to reveal a stock of tinned meats - this was obviously a regular service provided along with transport. We set off through the bush on the way to the "six-miler" and the foreman told the driver to stop when he saw a 40-gallon drum at the side of the road. We got out, hands full of tins, then set off in the dark, through the bush.

When I asked how he knew where we were going, I was told: "No worries, we should see his fire soon". Sure enough, we soon saw a flicker of flame and I discovered that Steve was living in a tent with his Aboriginal wife and son. Steve's own racing horse had the comfort of his own horse-box! The old stockman was also there, presumably with his own tent unless he slept under the stars. After a couple of hours drinking Old Soldier Rum, eating Spam out of the tin and seeing who could jump the furthest, which was the only thing to do, we made our way back to the road and waited for one of the passing taxis which apparently ran all night. We arrived back at Wyndham and I made my way back along the wharf to the ship, keeping a weather eye open for saltwater crocodiles.

We finally sailed from Wyndham on August 16, three days ahead of schedule, bound for Colombo where discharge of cargo was to take less than a day. Then, we would go on to Aden and the Red Sea. The strong wind, blowing from the African shore, seemed full of sand, which was stinging to the face as we steamed towards our Suez Bay anchorage, arriving in the early hours of September 3. The convoy left at 6am and we were in the Mediterranean by that evening.

We were on our berth in Liverpool by September 12 where the deck crew paid off, only to join a seaman's strike that had been going on for some time. I enjoyed a few evenings at home before being joined by a scratch crew of Captains' and Mates' tickets, including my old friend Mike Coghlan, who were to man the moorings fore and aft as we took the ship up to Glasgow. When we got there, we paid off but remained with the ship until signing on home-trade articles three days later for the coastal voyage down to London. I was finally able to start my leave on September 24, say hello to my new car and join the boy-racer club!

By mid-October, I was back at the Victoria Docks in London, to rejoin my ship and work by until we sailed again on November 18 on our way back to Australia, arriving at Port Said for the Canal transit. Having had our departure from London delayed by days of heavy rain, we had raced through the Mediterranean at up to 20 knots, increasing our fuel consumption by about 10 per cent to 44 tons per day trying to make the morning convoy - but to no avail.

We did make the afternoon convoy and after proceeding at full speed to Aden, then Ceylon, we finally arrived at Fremantle only a couple of days behind our original schedule. In the event, there was no berth for us and we had to spend a couple of days swinging at anchor. This also meant that we lost another couple of days as the Christmas break was spent in port before we could finish discharging cargo and get back to sea in time for New Year. The compensation for all this delay was that for every Sunday and Public Holiday spent at sea, we got an extra day's pay; in fairness, though, watch-keeping is a seven-day-a-week job, so we surely earnt it.

The ship's Captain, mellowed by having his wife aboard for the voyage, was a keen card player. After dinner in the evening, he and the Second Mate, together with the ship's doctor, would congregate in the Officers' smoke room for a game of pontoon or poker - I would be " requested" to join them to make up the numbers. Not being a natural gambler, I was always a cautious player and never ended up either winning or losing much, but both the Captain and Second Mate fancied their chances, with the older and more wily Captain generally coming out on top. There were occasions when I was really quite pleased to have to leave at 8pm for my evening watch on the bridge, when the First Mate would probably have to take my seat.

He was from Edinburgh and had taken exception to me signing notes organising table tennis and darts tournaments and the like on the ship's noticeboard as Third Mate, suggesting that, in Shaw Savill Line, I was "Third Officer' not 'Third Mate'. This was a rather snobbish attitude as our Certificates of Competency were as Mate and Master.

Sure enough, we were in Melbourne for January 2 and, while it was not quite as hot as the 105 degrees we had seen in Fremantle, the temperature occasionally reached 100 degrees. At that point, the dockers would stop work as it was too hot. On one such occasion, with nothing to do, I went to the local beach at St Kilda, got changed into my swimming trunks in the changing rooms, but ended up with burnt feet as soon as I walked onto the hot sand. A few days later, the temperature had dropped to a more moderate 70 degrees. Then, of course, the dockers carried on working, so no more beach. Not that I minded - after all that hot weather, it now seemed quite cold for our white tropical uniforms.

We had carried a small cargo of five dogs to Australia, which were looked after during the voyage by our apprentices. Two had gone ashore in Fremantle, one of which was claimed to be one of only 90 English Mastiffs left in the world, while one had left us in Melbourne; the remaining two little terriers bound for Sydney had now produced five little balls of fur with little pink faces and paws, which would earn the company another £4 for each puppy delivered alive. Business is business!

We arrived in Sydney on January 9; the weather had become a little more summery again and I could fulfil another ambition by going to the beautiful Bondi Beach for a swim. There were lots of bathers there but it was noticeable that none swam out beyond the breakers. This was not surprising as there seemed to be frequent reports on the radio of attacks on bathers by sharks.

I also took the opportunity of visiting the Caribbean Coffee Bar to see the owner's deaf son, Victor, the night before we left; while there, I met another eight friends of his who were all deaf and dumb. An exhausting time followed as they started asking me questions about the ship and England. One of them had only arrived in Australia six weeks before, from London. I also met Victor's very pretty girlfriend Helen, who could hear perfectly. I learned that his sister had married and he had become an uncle since my last visit.

We sailed early on Saturday morning to earn another weekend at sea and arrived in Brisbane for an early start on Monday to complete discharge in just two days, before leaving for Auckland in New Zealand, where we arrived on January 21 1961, ready to start loading for home. Whilst there, I visited an old shipmate from my time on the cadet ship in the Elder Dempster Line; he was then Second Mate with the coastal company Union Steamship and living in a rented flat in Auckland with his wife Rosemary and their eight-month-old baby. As I recall, Dick had emigrated to avoid marriage but Rosemary had followed him out to New Zealand and got her man after all, so persistence obviously paid off. They were due home in September so that Dick could return to college for his Master's ticket and they were both looking forward to that. I also managed to sell a couple of transistor radios and a pair of binoculars, which I had purchased in Aden early in the voyage so, both socially and financially, this had been a successful return to Auckland.

Wellington followed and then we were back up to the port of Napier, where the weather was idyllic and the people so friendly. After work had finished for the day, we would play cricket on the wharf and swim, although this was often in order to retrieve the ball after a particularly wild attempt at a boundary. The water was beautifully clear and we didn't need much encouragement, especially as, for some reason the water around New Zealand didn't seem to suffer the same shark hazard as it did around Australia.

Napier had been the epicentre of an earthquake in the 1930's, when half the town was swallowed up. After it was over, the visiting ships which had put to sea for safety came back and supplied food and aid. A sister ship of the Karamea, named the Coptic, actually ran power lines ashore and provided emergency electric power. The old port was left with only a few feet of water and a whole new and modern port was built, surrounded by the black beaches which are a reminder of that terrible time. That help given by the visiting ships may explain why the locals were so friendly and hospitable.

We had returned to Wellington to complete loading, so there was no visit to the South Island this time, but that was not the reason for the air of gloom which descended over the ship while we were there. Our chief refrigerating engineer had been visiting a friend on the brand new company ship Icenic one evening, enjoying a few drinks. His locked cabin door the following morning had been put down to a lie-in following a heavy night, so his failure to return was not noticed before word was received that his body had been recovered from the harbour. Perhaps another one for the road had been one too many, but it was a sad end to thirty years at sea which had seen him survive World War Two and finally be buried in New Zealand.

We left Wellington on February 22, made a quick call into Albany in Western Australia to top up our freshwater tanks and were in Aden by March 14 for bunkers. We would be at our first port of discharge in a mere three days.

Aqaba lies at the head of the Gulf of Aqaba, on the Jordanian side of the border with Israel and opposite the Jewish holiday resort of Eilat. It was made famous by Lawrence of Arabia, who led an army of tribesmen to defeat the Turks and win it back for the King of Jordan. As a port, it was not the sort of place where you would want to go ashore even if you had had the necessary permission, which we didn't. The 324-ton consignment of meat that we discharged overnight was apparently all to feed the troops of the Jordanian Army, who must have been hungry as there were heavily-armed men overseeing all the work.

Instead, our free time was spent having a musical soiree thanks to a young Glaswegian engineer who played guitar and various other home-made instruments such as a tea-chest bass. Aqaba was still worth seeing, as was the barren coastline which continued all the way back down the Sinai Peninsula to the Red Sea, where we altered course to starboard the following morning on our way up the Gulf of Suez and to the Suez Canal.

Once clear of Port Said, course was set to the south of Crete before passing through the Straits of Messina during the early-morning watch. However at 9am, just an hour into my watch, we passed the island of Stromboli and could clearly see the smoke coming from this active volcano as we made our way up to Genoa, where I had paid off the Bimini in the late-summer of 1958 on my way home after a 14-month voyage. Again, it was only a brief stay and a week later, on April 1 1961, I was paid off in my own home port of Liverpool, just in time for a few end-of-season games of rugby. I was particularly glad to go on leave from Liverpool as I was coming home with a frozen lamb carcass over my shoulder which had cost me £1 in New Zealand. Mother's friendly butcher separated it into joints and chops which were spread around the family.

There was a relief crew for the coastal voyage to London, where I rejoined my ship and signed on for my third consecutive voyage on the same ship, in itself a new experience for me. It would be similar to the last but a little shorter as we sailed on April 27 without a full cargo, at only 4,200 tons and alas, without the benefit of a Fourth Mate, making a little more work for the rest of us.

These outward voyages were beginning to feel like routine, with Port Said on May 6, then Aden four days later, although the boredom was broken on my birthday when I had a little bash, entertaining the Captain, Mate, Second Mate, Chief Engineer, Third Engineer, Chief Refrigerating Engineer, Chief Electrician, Radio Operator and Chief Steward. All it cost was a duty-free bottle of rum and a case of beer. We all had a pleasant social drink and everyone turned up for their watch on time. Most of us had been shipmates now for over a year. We all got on and worked well together and it had become a happy ship.

Following the seaman's strikes of the previous year, the deckhands seemed to get a reasonable pay increase The officers did not, so I purchased another three transistor radios and another pair of binoculars in Aden in an effort to make a difference. On arrival at Melbourne, we discovered that loading the homeward cargo would start again in Auckland, so I stowed them away until arrival in New Zealand.

Loading in Melbourne was not without incident, as I had to call for an ambulance twice whilst duty officer for the evening. The first time, it was one of the deck crew who arrived back at the ship along with a rather effeminate crew member of another ship in the port. The latter was tenderly bathing a deep cut in his nose, which had been sustained in a fight and which obviously required stitches. I hate to imagine what the fight had been about, but it seemed obvious at the time. The second time was when the Chief Engineer fell down a ladder, presumably after a drink too many.

We had a crew who were largely from Ulster. Sadly, they were more prone to the demon drink rearing its head in the form of violence than other crews I had sailed with, although they were mainly decent and cheerful with a great sense of humour. Like most crews, they were generally sober when at sea.

We discharged the rest of our cargo in Sydney, Brisbane and a place called Newcastle, which is quite close to Sydney. Whilst ashore there, I found a shop selling native spears and boomerangs. I bought a couple of the latter; they had probably never seen a native Aborigine but it still gave me some pleasure years later, when working in Newcastle, Northumberland to produce them and watch the faces when I said they had been bought in Newcastle, New South Wales!

I arrived in Auckland again on June 21 to find that my friend Dick Hayton had left the Union Steamship Company and bought a small grocery shop. His wife Rosemary now had a job as a doctor's receptionist. Things were not easy and with baby Alex, they were stuck at home most of the time, but optimistic that things would get better. Dreams of a Master's ticket had obviously been forgotten or put on hold. It was quite cold now in New Zealand and we were having something of a monsoon season for rain.

It was to put us a week or so behind schedule by the time we were in New Plymouth, which was a truly beautiful place with the snow-topped Mount Egmont rising 8,000 feet in the background. Whilst there, the Second Electrician hired a car and along with one of the Engineers, we set off after lunch on the Saturday afternoon and took a trip around the mountain, then followed signs to a place called Dawson Falls and found a hotel which described itself as a hostel. It was located about 3,000 feet up and right on the snow line. They had accommodation and we decided to stop there for the night.

We were not the only guests and found ourselves the object of some after-dinner curiosity. Eventually, a couple of girls from this quite young group came over and asked if we were from the Government Tourist Bureau, having checked in with cameras slung round our necks. They were, in fact, members of the New Zealand Young Conservatives and one of the two enquirers was Miss Diane Holyoak, daughter of the Prime Minister. Being of a British ship seemed to be just as good, for we had the girls' attention all evening to the apparent annoyance of the young men in the party. When I was introduced to Diane's boyfriend, I did a double-take as he was the image of my old friend, Mike Coghlan. Later, they took us down the mountain to a local dance, held in what seemed to be a gymnasium, but the thing that seemed most strange was that nobody took any notice of their Prime Minister's daughter, who could have been anyone.

There was also a fellow staying there from Liverpool who had emigrated with his wife and two children to work as a labourer three years before and was now selling advertising space. His 24-year-old boss was also staying there but if there was any connection with the other guests, it was not apparent. It was too wet to attempt to ski and after another few hours in friendly company, we left for the journey back to New Plymouth and our ship.

It took us over a week to complete loading in Bluff, which was on the southern tip of South Island. We left on July 21, bound for Aden and the longest stretch of the journey home. After only about seven hours, we were leaving Aden on the way up the Red Sea for another brief overnight stop at Aqaba. Apparently, they only work there during the cooler night hours and I couldn't blame them as the days were so hot.

After an evening transit, we were back in the Mediterranean by August 16 and on our way to the port of Pyraeus in Greece. Our berth was in easy walking distance of the yacht harbour and sitting outside a waterside café, sipping a cold Greek beer whilst admiring beautiful yachts and beautiful women, was a world away from the sort of scenery around dock areas of Liverpool and London. The actual Aegean Sea seemed even bluer than the Adriatic, even though both were part of the Mediterranean itself.

The Second Mate, Barry, and I decided to visit Athens, which was only about four miles away, so we hired a car and driver. The city itself, not just the royal and municipal buildings, seemed to be built entirely of stone and marble. Set off by the sunshine and blue sky it was most impressive, with none of the industrial grime that most of our cities seem to suffer from.

The culmination of our day had of course to be a tour of the Acropolis, built on the top of a hill which had in its time been the Royal Palace, a holy place and now one of the world's prime tourist attractions, built almost entirely of marble. The high wall around must have made it impregnable, with the Parthenon being the highest building within it. Although the front of the building still supported what seemed to be part of the roof, the side walls had almost collapsed to form two giant stairways to the top and I found the temptation too much to bear. Handing my camera to Barry, I stepped over the low rail and almost ran up the wall until I was standing on the very top of "the roof" enjoying the most magnificent view of the city from above, at which point I was distracted by whistles and shouts from the ground. As the person making all the noise was in uniform, I went back the way I had come to face a barrage of Greek. When I politely said that I didn't understand and asked if he could speak English, there was a look of exasperation and the words: " You English". I nodded an affirmative and he turned away with a shrug, muttering: "English".

In retrospect, I can only think that we still had some kudos from the war, otherwise I could well have spent the night in a Greek jail. It was no consolation at the time to find that my friend Barry had not taken the opportunity of taking a couple of photographs with my camera. That really would have made a memorable souvenir.

After that little adventure, we left Piraeus for another brief stay at Genoa, where I purchased several boxes of their famous Merino wool blankets, before arriving back in the Victoria dock, London and then paying off on August 30 to start my leave. The ship followed me to Liverpool a couple of weeks later which saved me having to travel by train with all my treasures, including the blankets, which were circulated as presents around the family.

# CHAPTER 23 - SECOND MATE ONCE MORE

Just over three weeks later, I was back in the same dock to join my new ship Cedric, in good spirits because at last I had my promotion to Second Mate again, the rank I had left when I paid off the Bimini almost three years before. My new rate of pay was a magnificent £1,000 per year but I was to have more to contend with than the graveyard watch from midnight to four in the morning and the afternoon watch when everybody else was able to take their afternoon siesta at sea. I was now the navigating officer at sea, responsible for altering all the clocks on the ship as we passed through time zones and also in charge of completing all the cargo plans when we were loading the homeward cargo. To put a top hat on it, I discovered that our Captain was the same 'Bastard' that I had sailed with on the Karamea. Later on in the voyage, I was answering a question about navigation, put to me by the apprentice on my watch, when the Captain appeared on the bridge and suggested that I was not there to chatter. When I followed him to his cabin behind the bridge and angrily told him what the "chatter" was about, he at least had the grace to apologise; relations between us seemed to improve from that point on.

*MV Cedric*

I was to have a taste of the extra duties that being Second Mate involved, even before we left at 1am the next morning, laying courses off on our charts, from the Thames all the way round to Gibraltar, then on to Suez ready for the Canal transit. After letting go the moorings and clearing the dock, I would be back on the bridge as we steamed down river until 4 am when I came off watch.

As soon as we were out of sight of land, as navigating officer I was back on the bridge after breakfast to take a morning altitude of the sun, which would give a position line which I could cross with a latitude at noon, or when the sun was at its highest point, to give a noon position. The Captain and the Third Mate would also have taken sights and these would be compared before the Captain decided exactly where our true position was and adjusted our course accordingly. By that time, I was already on watch again until 4pm.

Before leaving London, we would also have received the latest pile of "notices to mariners" which advised all the known changes to our world charts. Over the next few weeks, whenever I had a free moment, I would have to make the appropriate alterations to our charts so that they were accurate. This was another of the laborious duties that would fill my time. At least it made the hours pass more quickly, although I could have found a more pleasant way of achieving that objective.

Another job which always seemed to land on my desk was the preparation of cargo summaries, using all the cargo notes and plans left with us by the company stevedores in London. There was a 'disposition of cargo' list, a list of heavy weights and so on, all to allow us to open the right hatches in the right ports and discharge the correct cargo in the shortest time. Being new to all these extra duties made them take longer; I improved as time went on but when I compared all this with the comparatively easy life of some of the other engineers and officers, life seemed somewhat unfair. Hopefully, this voyage would provide me with enough sea-time to qualify for a return to college for my Master's ticket and then a cushy shore job!

In no time, we had cleared the Suez Canal, bunkered at Aden (where I purchased an 8mm movie camera for £27, a lot of money in 1961) and crossed the Indian Ocean. By the end of October, we were in Melbourne. I was finding the work easier by now and presumably doing it well, with a decent working relationship with our Captain who had spent the voyage so far taking it out on the poor young Fourth Mate. My time off duty was usually spent with our newly promoted Third Mate, Stan. As they were both relatively inexperienced, I spent most of my time on board when cargo was being worked and I supposed I had done the sightseeing bit.

The weather was quite cool for November and cargo-work was badly disrupted by monsoon-type rain, especially in Sydney where, as soon as it started, the dockers would walk off the ship and leave us to close the hatches. Although we had McGregor Hatch lids, which only involved using a winch to draw the lids across, we would still be soaking wet after keeping our cargo dry in five or six hatches. These delays also caused us to sometimes leave port without completing discharge and much shifting cargo around. Days were lost and wages still had to be paid for dockworkers as they played cards etc. in the canteen.

It was the usual ports round to Brisbane before we prepared the holds and started loading our homeward cargo in Tasmania. First, we went to a small place with the name of Beauty Point on the Tamar River, which goes up to Launceston. Not that we saw much of it apart from the local pub in the evening. The locals were quite friendly, especially one who seemed to be an engineer with a very understanding, or perhaps patient, wife. When the pub closed, he invited all of us back to his house for some supper.

Supper turned out to be another beer. His wife must have been somewhat relieved when he took us into the large wooded garage at the side of the house to show us his pride and joy. It was a home-built autogyro which he swore had flown, albeit only a short distance, along his road. The helicopter-like blades had been removed and were hanging on the wall but the small home-made wooden propeller was in place behind the lawn-mower engine fixed to the back of the small fuselage. The latter resembled a large baby's pram, which it probably was.

He insisted that I sat in the pilot seat to try it for size before he started the engine. A set of handlebars had been used to steer it when on the ground and to move the flaps and rudders. What he hadn't shown me was the small throttle which he took great pleasure in flipping to full power. To my horror, as the flying machine started to move I realised that there seemed to be no brakes. It was a large garage-cum-workshop and, facing the large closed doors, I could only swing the steering from side-to-side to slow down the machine before it came to rest hard against them. He, and the rest of my shipmates, thought it a great joke. He stopped the engine and I hastily climbed out. By this time, his wife was losing patience so we bid farewell and beat a retreat back to the ship. Loading was largely to be in Melbourne after calls at Burnie and Portland, with Fremantle the final port of loading this trip after another brief call at Albany for more bales of wool.

Sailing day from the final port of loading was an extremely tense time for the Second Mate. The large cargo plan, coloured differently for each port of discharge, had to be completed not once but using two different pads, each about three feet by two feet wide, with enough carbon copies for up to ten ports plus extra copies for Head Office and so on. These had to be taken ashore for posting before the ship sailed and, with work only just completed and the Captain drumming his fingers on the desk and anxious not to lose any more time, stress levels were at new heights. I finished typing out the cargo summaries while the apprentices finished colouring and it was a relief to join the crew aft at stations, ready to let go moorings, say what was to be a final goodbye to Australia and start the long trip home.

It was Boxing Day 1961 and my final visit to Aden in the Yemen for bunkers. My present to myself was to buy my last transistor radio there, one with a long wave band instead of a short wave, ready for the Light Programme when I got home. It had been a relief to arrive in Aden as the crew, or at least the Ulster element, had celebrated Christmas in riotous fashion with a final score of three cracked ribs and bad cuts for one of the engine-room greasers, a cook's finger almost bitten off with the chief cook's wrist broken, half-a-dozen bruised jaws and as many sprained wrists and fingers, not to mention a cabin door smashed in with a meat cleaver.

We had just 62 tons of cargo for Port Said, mainly bales of wool, after we got through the Canal. We then proceeded to Genoa to discharge another 391 tons, mainly wool with some egg pulp in cartons. From there, we sailed to London where I signed off on January 20, only to sign on again 438 tons and six days later for the coastal voyage to Dunkirk, back across the North Sea to Hull and then to Antwerp, before finally arriving back in London where I eventually paid off on February 14 1962.

Sadly, I was still a couple of weeks short of the requisite amount of seatime that would enable me to take my Master's ticket but I was able to sign on another company ship called the Cymric, which was in the same dock two days later, for a short coastal trip to mainland Europe and back. Returning to the ship after a few drinks ashore with the First Mate, we smelt smoke and after obtaining the keys, opened a hatch to discover a fire down in the shelter deck. The steel deck was still covered in a layer of sawdust, laying under a temporary wood floor, which had been used to insulate the frozen cargo in the tweed deck beneath. The smoke was coming from a small area of this sawdust, which had probably ignited from a discarded cigarette end. The Fire Brigade were called in line with ship's orders but, by the time they arrived, we had doused the area with a fire extinguisher and all they had to do was certify that the danger was passed.

Another quick trip across the North Sea and back saw me with enough sea time and I paid off what was to be my last ship, back in Victoria Docks, London on March 1 1962. I travelled home and after a short break, registered once more at the Nautical College in Liverpool. There, I started the three-month preparatory course prior to taking the exam to gain a Certificate of Competency as Master Mariner. This time, I was to receive three months' extra wages from my employers.

## CERTIFICATE OF COMPETENCY

AS

# MASTER

OF A FOREIGN-GOING STEAMSHIP     No.93363

To   *George    Edward    Dickinson*

WHEREAS you have been found duly qualified to fulfil the duties of Master of a Foreign-going Steamship in the Merchant Service, the Minister of Transport in exercise of his powers under the Merchant Shipping Acts and of all other powers enabling him in that behalf, hereby grants you this Certificate of Competency.

SIGNED BY AUTHORITY OF THE MINISTER OF TRANSPORT and dated this     *4th*

day of *October* 19*62*

Countersigned

Registrar General

A Deputy Secretary of the Ministry of Transport

REGISTERED AT THE OFFICE OF THE REGISTRAR GENERAL OF SHIPPING AND SEAMEN

# CHAPTER 24 - BACK TO COLLEGE

As on previous occasions, I was able to catch the rest of the rugby season, not to mention the party season, so I was determined to make up for lost time. I had a nice car, the boot of which was always prepared with a small crate of ale and either Babycham or some other suitable drink for the ladies plus, of course, a supply of cigarettes. I suppose it was the old Scouts motto of "Be Prepared" which I had never forgotten. I had found my girlfriend and future wife, who patiently spent hours sitting in a secluded spot while she tested me on 'Rules for the Prevention of Collision at Sea' etc and was taking life easy. Too easy as, by the time I had sat all my exams and finally qualified, I was back living on my savings.

This was perhaps unfair as it was only then that I informed my Company that I had decided to leave the sea and take a shore job, with marriage firmly in mind. As already noted, I had met June, the light of my life, some months before and on the day my results came through, we set off in my new Ford Anglia for a short holiday in Devon and Cornwall, before I proposed and gained the approval of my future father-in-law. Having achieved that, I actually started to look for a job ashore. There was something of a recession in the winter of 1962/63 and job-hunting proved much harder that I thought.

My friend and future best man still worked for a marine paint company in Liverpool and this seemed the sort of work that an ex-Merchant Navy Officer would be quite suited to. But it was March 1963, just three weeks after June and I got married, that I moved to Newcastle-on-Tyne to start my first shore job.

*The Author and his bride June on their wedding day*

# CHAPTER 25 - MY NEW CAREER

International Paints Limited were the largest supplier of ships' paint in the world, with their UK factory on the River Tyne, but I was to be based at the Newcastle city office along with a senior colleague, under the control of a technical manager based in the head office in London. I had been given to understand that my work would be in shipyards and drydocks all over the UK, but mainly on the Tyne, with occasional jobs overseas. I soon learnt that I was to travel a lot more than that.

My first job overseas was to a ship in Malta and then on to Marseilles for another ship. I travelled home as soon as possible, but was still in London making my report to Head Office when Andrew was born in Southport. I was able to make it home to be the first visitor before we both returned to our little bungalow in West Monkseaton, near Whitley Bay.

I would often work closely with the research and development department and oversee trials of new materials at a time of many advances in cargo coatings and antifouling; but time at home became less and less and work in sales seemed much more conducive with married life, especially when more children came along, as Simon did. We were still living in west Monkseaton and he was born in Tynemouth Hospital - it was still the first visiting time before I was able to see them both. Fathers were still considered a nuisance at the birth in those days.

After three years, I changed my employer early in 1966 and moved back to Liverpool to work with my old friend Des Laidler at Red Hand Compositions Company, part of the Courtaulds Group. A couple of years later, they bought my old company and I found myself working for International Red Hand.

I had been carrying out both sales and technical work in Liverpool, with the odd trip to a shipyard away from the Mersey, when I was offered a move to East Anglia. June and I now had three sons, Andrew, Simon and Jamie, who was born in the Liverpool Maternity Hospital. We bought a house in a small village called Belton, just outside Great Yarmouth and spent eight happy years there with the boys attending the local schools.

I was manager for East Anglia and had an exciting time working in the small shipyards and in the growing offshore industry, eventually being responsible for all our offshore business in the UK. As the centre for this business moved up to Scotland and I did not want to move with it, I transferred to our Yacht Department and spent the rest of my time there working with things like racing yachts; an area in which even more technical advances were being made in a much more pleasant environment.

Eventually, we moved to Southampton, which was the centre of this business. My area included the Channel Islands and Cowes, on the Isle of Wight. We bought a house on the outskirts of the city and both Andrew and Simon attended the Mountbatten School in Romsey. For me, happy days were spent in the summer sunshine at marinas around the Solent and attending boat shows until, five years later, the Company offered me a job back in Marine Division as North West Area Manager, based at our old office in Liverpool. Andrew was already at the Manchester Polytechnic, now part of Manchester University and Simon joined him there by the time we had finally moved house. Jamie was able to attend a school near by where he took his A levels and then started work.

This was a move back home, near to our families, which I gratefully accepted, although I was to witness the fall of Liverpool as a major seaport and end my working life operating from an office at my home. I retired in 1996 and we have remained here ever since, in the town I where I was born.

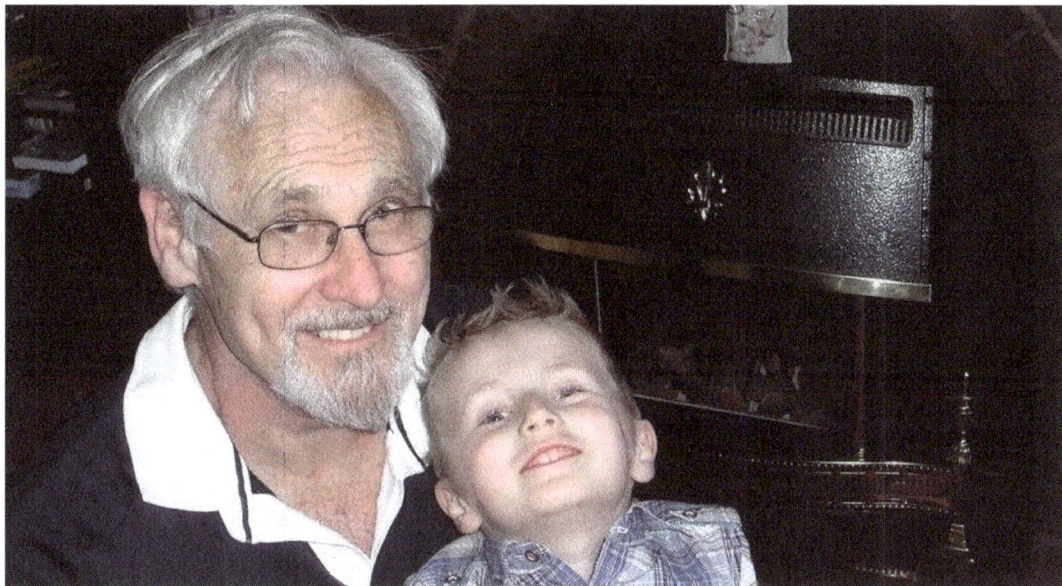

*Above Jacob, the Author's first grandchild and Below all four grandchildren, Jacob, Lewis, Daisy and Emily*

# THE SEAGOING CAREER OF ED DICKINSON (1952 - 1962)

| | | JOINED | LEFT | VOYAGE | DAYS LEAVE |
|---|---|---|---|---|---|
| **Elder Dempster Line, (Apprenticeship Dec 1952 - Dec 1956)** | | | | | |
| Tarkwa | Apprentice | Dec 16 | Feb 21 | 2 m 5 d | 11 |
| Tarkwa | " | Mar 4 | May 8 | 2 m 4 d | 6 |
| Fulani | " | May 14 | Aug 20 | 3 m 6 d | 19 |
| David Livingstone | | Sept 8 | Sept 11 | 3 d | 0 |
| Cambray | " | Sept 11 | Oct 19 | 1 m 8 d | 0 |
| Eboe | " | Oct 20 | May 7 | 6 m 18 d | 22 |
| Zini | " | May 29 | Feb 8 | 8 m 10 d | 7 |
| Swedru | " | Feb 15 | Aug 31 | 6 m 6 d 19 | |
| Accra | " | Sept 19 | Oct 24 | 1 m 5 d | 8 |
| Obuasi | " | Nov 1 | Dec 15 | 1 m 14 d | |
| Operation for acute appendicitis at Creek Hospital, Lagos | | | | | 7 |
| Apapa | Passenger | Dec 22 | Dec 26 | | |
| Accra | Apprentice | Jan 17 | Feb 28 | 1 m 11 d | 0 |
| Accra | " | Feb 28 | Apr 4 | 1 m 4 d | 15 |
| Obuasi | " | Apr 19 | Oct 30 | 6 m 11 d | 32 |
| Aureol | 4th Mate | Dec 1 | Jan 1 | 1 m 0 d | |

**STUDIES FOR SECOND MATE'S TICKET AT CLARENCE STREET, LIVERPOOL**
Passed May 30 1957

| **Ante Topic Line (Foreign Flag)** | | | | | |
|---|---|---|---|---|---|
| Panamante | 3rd Mate | June 24 | Apr 30 | 10 m 6 d | 0 |
| Bimini | 2nd Mate | May 1 | Aug 30 | 3 m 30 d | |

**STUDIES FOR FIRST MATE'S TICKET AT BYROM STREET, LIVERPOOL**
Passed April 2 1959

| **Shaw Savill Line** | | | | | |
|---|---|---|---|---|---|
| Delphic | 4th Mate | Apr 13 | Sept 20 | 5 m 7 d | 27 |
| Athenic | 4th Mate | Oct 17 | Oct 17 | | |
| Karamea | 3rd Mate | Oct 17 | Mar 20 | | |
| Canopic | 3rd Mate | Apr 14 | Sept 24 | | |
| Canopic | 3rd Mate | Nov 16 | Apr 1 | | |
| Canopic | 3rd Mate | Apr 26 | Aug 30 | | |
| Cedric | 2nd Mate | Sept 27 | Feb 14 | | |
| Cymric | 2nd Mate | Feb 16 | Mar 1 | | |

**STUDIES FOR MASTER'S TICKET AT BYROM STREET, LIVERPOOL**
Passed 1962    Oct 4

**QUALIFICATION AS MASTER MARINER DATED OCTOBER 10TH 1962**

www.ingramcontent.com/pod-product-compliance
Lightning Source LLC
Chambersburg PA
CBHW060756150426
42811CB00058B/1428